Eric Clapton

D0732572

the Complete Guide *to his* Music

OMNIBUS PRESS
London/New York
Paris/Sydney/Copenhagen
Berlin/Madrid/Tokyo

Marc Roberty

Cover and book designed by Chloë Alexander
Cover image courtesy of Nicholas Burnham/Retna

ISBN: 1.84609.007.5
Order No: OP 51062

Exclusive Distributors
Music Sales Limited,
8/9 Frith Street,
London W1D 3JB, UK.

Music Sales Corporation,
257 Park Avenue South,
New York, NY 10010, USA.

Macmillan Distribution Services,
53 Park West Drive,
Derrimut, Vic 3030,
Australia.

To the Music Trade only:
Music Sales Limited,
8/9 Frith Street,
London W1D 3JB, UK.

Every effort has been made to trace the copyright holders
of the photographs in this book but one or two were
unreachable. We would be grateful if the photographers
concerned would contact us.

Printed and bound in Great Britain by Mackays of Chatham plc, Chatham, Kent

A catalogue record for this book is available from the
British Library.

Visit Omnibus Press on the web at
www.omnibuspress.com

Contents

INTRODUCTION

ERIC CLAPTON WAS NEVER A SPOKESMAN FOR HIS GENERATION LIKE John Lennon or Pete Townshend, never an alchemist like Jimi Hendrix or Jimmy Page, or even a speed technician like Jeff Beck or Ritchie Blackmore. Instead, his emotions and thoughts were channelled to the tips of his fingers, and he became a guitar god to many generations through his ability to interpret black man's blues to young white audiences.

Eric's phenomenal longevity was confirmed in 1993 with multiple Grammy Awards for current and past achievements. It was also the year Eric returned again to the crossroads, the mythical moment of decision that all artists must face from time to time. He'd travelled down each and every one of those roads with mixed results over the years but now, at last, he felt comfortable enough with himself to return to the cradle: the blues.

Eric's journey has been long and varied. His first recordings were with The Yardbirds, the influential Sixties R&B group that is now remembered largely for their trio of stellar guitarists. Sadly, Eric's record-ed output with them was only a handful of demos, studio singles and live shows. He left after the recording of the quintet's first hit, 'For Your Love' because he felt they were becoming too commercial and betray-ing their blues roots.

He was not unemployed for long. John Mayall installed Eric in his Bluesbreakers and together they went on to produce *the* seminal British blues album of the Sixties, but Eric soon tired of copying his heroes and sought a new outlet. After briefly playing with Jack Bruce in the Blues-breakers he approached him to propose forming a new group with drummer Ginger Baker.

They called themselves Cream. Eric once referred to them as a glo-rious mistake. He had envisaged a kind of Buddy Guy trio with Eric lead-ing a British improvisatory blues band. Instead, they were the leading lights of underground pop – or rock as it became known – in the late Sixties and led the way for all power trios of the future. A bright star that was extinguished after only two years, they left behind three and a bit studio albums and several posthumous live sets. By selling their soul to the great Yankee dollar, they paid the ultimate price: US tours of huge magnitude crippled them and stifled creativity. Their acrimonious split left scars that still smarted 25 years later, although they re-united briefly in 1993 for the Rock'n'Roll Hall of Fame Awards. But then, in 2005, the unthinkable happened. Cream reformed for an exclusive run of four shows at the Royal Albert Hall, the very venue at which they played their last gig. As soon as the three of them started rehearsals, the old magic came back.

Eric soaked up many influences on his visits to America with Cream, none more so than The Band. In an attempt to somehow emulate them, he and Stevie Winwood, together with Ginger Baker and Rick Grech, formed one of the first "supergroups" and called themselves Blind Faith. This time Eric envisaged an American sound but he was thwarted from the start by fans who wanted only to hear the music of Cream and Traffic. Their eponymous album remains the sole memento of a group that offered much but were unable to deliver due to the pressures of the media and public.

As a means of temporary escape from the limelight, Eric rather naïvely joined up with Delaney & Bonnie Bramlett as a sideman while deciding on his future. Together they recorded a studio single as well as a live album from a show at Croydon's Fairfield Hall. Delaney produced Eric's first solo album which was followed by a rather half-hearted attempt at anonymity in Derek and The Dominos, who comprised some of Delaney & Bonnie's band. Certainly one of his best bands, this tight unit recorded one of the Seventies' truly classic albums, *Layla And Other Assorted Love Songs*, but the initial failure of the album, together with mounting personal and drug problems, forced Eric into self-imposed seclusion.

He re-emerged in the mid-Seventies as a solo performer backed by strong bands which he would periodically change to keep his ideas fresh, and his status as a senior journeyman in the rock world has gained authority with each passing year. Some of his later music has been criticised for being lightweight, for lacking inspiration, and for straying too far from his blues roots, but at the very heart of Eric Clapton is a steely professionalism – perhaps instilled by that old sage John Mayall – which has ensured that Eric Clapton always delivers.

Each year thousands turn out to see Eric at his now traditional season of Royal Albert Hall shows, and his 1992 *Unplugged* album of songs performed for the popular MTV series became his best-selling album ever. In recent years he has released several commercial pop albums that continue to keep him in the public eye. A surprise album of Robert Johnson covers became a hugely successful album for him in 2004 and he toured the world to promote it. Eric is also proud to be a part of the 'establishment'. In 1994 the Queen granted him an Officer of the Order of the British Empire (OBE) for "contribution to British Life." Later, in 2004 Eric was honored by Queen Elizabeth II with the award of C.B.E. - Commander of the Order of the British Empire. He described it as "the icing on the cake" of his career.

In 2005, Eric's 60th year, he is busier than ever, performing at the RAH for a four-night season in May with the reformed Cream. Demand for tickets was unprecedented with prices pushing well over £1000 on the internet auction site, eBay. To capitalise on the interest, Universal released the TV-advertised collection, *I Feel Free – Ultimate Cream* a career-spanning collection highlighting both sides of the band – the wildly experimental studio outfit and the stripped-down live power trio. Aside from this, Eric plans to release a new pop album as well as planning a massive career-spanning DVD for 2006.

Like the blues heroes that inspired him to pick up a guitar in the first place, Eric Clapton seems likely to be making music well into his old age.

If you are a new admirer I hope this book will help guide you in the direction of Eric's better work and if you are an old fan, it might inspire you to dig out and reassess some titles you may well not have heard in a while.

Marc Roberty,
May 2005

PART ONE
THE YARDBIRDS

I WISH YOU WOULD/ A CERTAIN GIRL
Columbia DB7283
released May 1964

ERIC'S FIRST appearance on record was a Billy Boy Arnold number by The Yardbirds, a regular stage favourite which appeared on the original demo tape that won them a record contract with EMI. A basic R&B song driven by Keith Relf's harmonica, recorded at the old Olympic Studios near Marble Arch, it didn't even make the Top Twenty.

The B-side 'A Certain Girl' is an altogether better proposition for Eric fans as it features a beautifully controlled guitar solo and is clearly the initiation for anyone starting a collection of memorable EC solos.

GOOD MORNING LITTLE SCHOOLGIRL/ I AIN'T GOT YOU
Columbia DB7391
released October 1964

THE YARDBIRDS' second single was chosen by Eric and came as close to a commercial sound that he felt comfortable with, while remaining true to his blues roots. With an acceptable guitar solo, 'Schoolgirl' chugs along with good vocals and harmonies but it still failed to capture their legendary live sound.

Eric's guitar solos were now relegated to Yardbirds' B-sides, and 'I Ain't Got You' features a blistering solo and is, in many respects, a better number than the A-side. With the benefit of hindsight, this may have had a greater chance of being a hit than the by now traditional blues standard on the A-side.

Five Live Yardbirds

Columbia 33SX 1677; released December 1964.
CD: Rhino 70189, October 1990

AFTER RECORDING SEVERAL DEMOS, MANAGER GOMELSKY SIGNED THE Yardbirds – Eric, Keith Relf (vocals), Chris Dreja (guitar), Paul Samwell-Smith (bass) and Jim McCarty (drums) – to a tape lease deal with EMI in February 1964. They recorded their first album live during their residency at London's Marquee in March 1964. By this time the group's club shows were already well established and a regular crowd would follow them wherever they played.

The R&B drenched set included numbers by Chuck Berry, Eddie Boyd, Chester Burnett and The Isley Brothers amongst others. The album *Five Live Yardbirds* captures the gig rather crudely, but the sweaty atmosphere is intact. It was perhaps short-sighted of EMI to release Yardbirds' studio singles first in an attempt to secure chart placings for their new protégés, when they were better known for their live shows on the London R&B circuit.

Another irony is that during playback of the two-track tapes, Paul Samwell-Smith accidentally erased several numbers, including a live version of their first single 'I Wish You Would'.

TOO MUCH MONKEY BUSINESS
(Berry)

"GOOD EVENING! And welcome! And now it is time for Bird-merising, Yardmerising... in fact, most blueswailing Yardbirds! Here they are one by one, the drums, Jim McCarty, the rhythm guitar, Chris Dreja, the bass Paul Samwell-Smith, lead guitar, Eric 'Slowhand' Clapton, the singer and harp Keith Relf....FIVE LIVE YARDBIRDS!!!" So goes Marquee M.C.'s Hamish Grimes' introduction to one of the most historic releases of British R&B, capturing, albeit rather crudely, one of the finest gigs by The Yardbirds, just as they sounded at London's Marquee Club one night in March 1964.

On the opening song they more than do justice to Chuck Berry's 'Too Much Monkey Busi-ness', a typical Yardbirds 'rave-up' of musical climaxes stretching from the bottom of the fretboard to the top and back down again, all designed to develop crowd frenzy from the get-go.

GOT LOVE IF YOU WANT IT
(Moore)

RAW R & B in this cover of Slim Harpo's classic, but no guitar solo.

SMOKESTACK LIGHTNING
(Burnett)

A BLUES staple by Howlin' Wolf – like 'Got Love If You Want It' covered by countless mid-60's British R&B bands – and a live favourite which gave Eric ample opportunity to show off his licks and crescendo chords, which clearly delighted the fans.

GOOD MORNING LITTLE SCHOOLGIRL
(Demarais)

ERIC GETS to sing a duet with 'Sam' (Samwell-Smith) on this high energy version of the group's second single, but there's no guitar break on this live version.

RESPECTABLE
(Isley/Isley/Isley)

THE YARDBIRDS often finished their first set with this Isley Brothers' number which features some wild playing by Eric. Halfway through, the arrangement segues into a rather jovial version of Derrick Morgan's ska novelty, 'Humpty Dumpty'.

FIVE LONG YEARS
(Boyd)

ERIC DEMONSTRATES his precocious talents as a blues player on a classic Eddie Boyd number which opens the second set and Side Two. Eric performed this number at several of his regular blues shows during the early Nineties at London's Royal Albert Hall.

PRETTY GIRL
(McDaniel)

KEITH WHIPS out his maracas for this typical Bo Diddley number, while Eric provides the usual adrenalin charged guitar chords which are spattered all over this live set.

LOUISE
(Hooker)

BIG FANS of John Lee Hooker, The Yardbirds play a passable version of this song and Eric boogies along accordingly.

I'M A MAN
(McDaniel)

A RATHER tame version compared to the frighteningly awesome Bo Diddley original and the lurching 'Maximum R&B' style of the newly emerging Who. However, these suburban white kids from Surrey played their hearts out as best they could, and for most people that was good enough.

HERE 'TIS
(McDaniel)

A NOTHER Bo Diddley song much covered by London's R&B bands and in The Yardbirds' hands it's just one more final 'rave-up' and they're off, leaving a great live album to treasure as a true memento of a period that can sadly never be recaptured.

FOR YOUR LOVE/ GOT TO HURRY
Columbia DB7499
released March 1965

A N HISTORIC Yardbirds' single for two reasons. Firstly, 'For Your Love' was a deliberate change in direction from blues to Gregorian chants packaged as commercial pop, and as a result Eric packed his bags, leaving Paul Samwell-Smith to take over as musical director. Eric appears only briefly on the bridge of the song which features a harpsichord as the dominant instrument. Written by Graham Gouldman, it reached number 3 in the UK charts in April '65, thus opening up a pop career for them. Eric had wanted to record Otis Redding's 'Your One And Only Man' as the A-side but was vetoed by the others.

Secondly, the B-side 'Got To Hurry', was the first song that Eric ever wrote, or at least his first composition to be recorded. A blues shuffle, it features stunning guitar lines played through a Vox amp cranked up to full volume with plenty of buzz and crackle now clearly audible on the digital format. Sadly, Eric was somehow talked out of his composer's credit on the label by manager Giorgio Gomelsky who used his own pseudonym 'Rasputin', a nickname the band had given him, as a way of collecting publishing royalties.

'Got To Hurry' was the performance that caught the attention of the guv'nor of Eric's next group.

Sonny Boy Williamson & The Yardbirds

Fontana TL5277, released 1966. CD: Sunspots, December 2003

RECORDED **LIVE AT THE CRAWDADDY CLUB, RICHMOND, SURREY, UK ON** 8 December, 1963. Produced by Giorgio Gomelsky, a nervous Yardbirds back blues harmonica player Sonny Boy Williamson. The original, mono Fontana TL5277 was reissued in stereo as SFJL960 and issued in the US as Mercury SR21071. The current 23 track Sunspots CD also features 'Highway '69' and 'My Little Cabin' recorded at the Birmingham R&B Festival in early 1964.

TRACKS: Bye Bye Bird, Pontiac Blues, Take It Easy Baby, I Don't Care No More, Mister Downchild, 23 Hours Too Long, Out On The Water Coast, Baby Don't Worry

Live! Blueswailing July '64

Castle CMQCD793, released September 2003

AN **AMAZING UNRELEASED LIVE RECORDING BY THE YARDBIRDS WHICH** is rumoured to be from a gig at The Cavern Club in Liverpool on July 5, 1964. It was also released on vinyl by Sundazed Records in the US.

SOMEONE TO LOVE ME
(Pryor)

ABRIEF but rousing opening cover of a Snooky Pryor song.

TOO MUCH MONKEY BUSINESS
(Berry)

ANOTHER typical Yardbirds "rave-up" of musical climaxes stretching from the bottom of the fretboard to the top and back down again. Eric plays a fiery solo.

GOT LOVE IF YOU WANT IT
(Moore)

THE ENERGY here is crackling and dangerous – the ultimate garage band.

SMOKESTACK LIGHTNING
(Burnett)

THE GROUP really roars through this one.

GOOD MORNING LITTLE SCHOOLGIRL
(Demarais)

HIGH energy version of the group's second single – not released until October.

RESPECTABLE/ HUMPTY DUMPTY
(Isley/Isley/Isley)

GREAT bass playing from 'Sam' on this one, skipping nimbly across the breakneck tempos of the Isley Brothers' 'Respectable', with usual blue beat segue into 'Humpty Dumpty'.

THE SKY IS CRYING
(James)

SIX MINUTE version of the Elmore James blues classic. Eric is in fine form sparring against Keith Relf's harmonica.

PART TWO

JOHN MAYALL'S BLUESBREAKERS

JOHN **M**AYALL **TRACKED** **E**RIC **DOWN** **AFTER** **READING** **ABOUT** **HIS** **DEPARTURE** from The Yardbirds in *Melody Maker*. Mayall had heard Eric's guitar on 'Got To Hurry', the B-side of 'For Your Love', and he desperately wanted him to replace the outgoing Roger Dean in the Bluesbreakers. Eric was asked to join immediately after his audition and he felt instantly at home in a non-commercial blues-based environment.

At that time – the spring of 1965 – the Bluesbreakers consisted of Mayall on guitar, keyboards and vocals, Eric on guitar and vocals, John McVie on bass, and Hughie Flint on drums, but during Eric's sojourn in the band, Jack Bruce, a virtuoso Scottish bass player whose roots lay more in jazz than rock, would pass through the Bluesbreakers' ranks and leave a deep impression on their young guitarist.

No line-up of the Bluesbreakers ever seemed to last for very long. Mayall was probably the first British musician of appeal to rock fans who abandoned the concept of a stable group in favour of continuous change. He would surround himself with musicians of his choice, hiring and firing them almost at will, in much the same manner as jazz musicians, especially those leading small combos, had been doing for years. Eric stayed for just one album, recorded at Decca studios in Hampstead, and quit because the work rate imposed by Mayall left little time for fun. He also fancied the idea of teaming up with that Scottish fellow.

I'M YOUR WITCHDOCTOR/ TELEPHONE BLUES
Immediate IM012
released October 1965
(Mayall)

ERIC'S **FIRST** recording with John Mayall featured single note feedback solos. It was a promising début single which offered plenty of clues to the direction in which Eric was heading. The single was produced by Jimmy Page who, at the time was a top session player and in-house producer for Immediate.

LONELY YEARS/
BERNARD JENKINS
Purdah 3502
released August 1966

ONE OF Eric's rarest recordings: only 500 were pressed by Purdah, a small independent South London label set up by blues aficionado Mike Vernon who went on to form Blue Horizon, home to many seminal late-'60s British blues bands including Fleetwood Mac and Chicken Shack.

Recorded in Wessex Studios, Vernon successfully captured the authentic raw Chicago electric blues sound of the Fifties. The A-side features Mayall on harmonica and vocal accompanied by Eric's fluid guitar runs.

The B-side was a great boogie-woogie track with Mayall on piano and Eric providing some Freddie King style soloing over the top of it all. The B-side's rather unusual title came from the band's fondness for a current production of the Harold Pinter play *The Caretaker*. In it, a down-and-out played by Donald Pleasance attempts to infiltrate the home of two eccentric brothers. When asked his name, he blurts out "Bernard Jenkins."

John Mayall's Blues Breakers With Eric Clapton

Decca SKL4804; released July 1966
CD: Polygram 8448272, October 1990

ALL YOUR LOVE
(Rush)

ERIC GETS to be Otis Rush for this faithful copy. Rush was a major influence on Eric at the time and this track was among the many records in Mayall's vast blues collection which served as the main reference library for both their live set and studio recordings.

HIDEAWAY
(King, Thompson)

ANOTHER important early influence on Eric, Freddie King's style remains in his playing to this day. Eric's Gibson Les Paul drives the number along with Mayall playing some cool Hammond organ. This is really Eric's *tour de force* and a definite highlight on the album. Eric also played this number during Cream's 1968 US tour.

LITTLE GIRL
(Mayall)

A FAIRLY typical Mayall composition of the time, featuring Eric's fancy lead work in the left channel speaker. Listen out for some nice vibrato.

ANOTHER MAN
(arr. Mayall)

A HARMONICA led number with no discernible guitar. Maybe Eric contributes the handclaps!

DOUBLE CROSSIN' TIME
(Mayall, Clapton)

CO-WRITTEN by Eric, this dirty mean old electric blues is another Clapton extravaganza. This sound – his Gibson Les Paul played at concert pitch through a 50 watt Marshall amp and 4 x 12" speaker cabinet – revolutionised the sound of British blues playing, earlier attempts having been played through the boosted treble channels of Vox AC30 amps.

The song itself is a thinly disguised account of how Jack Bruce left the Mayall band to join the highly commercial Manfred Mann the previous year.

WHAT'D I SAY
(Charles)

A FAITHFUL copy of the very well-known Ray Charles classic that was being played by almost every British R&B band at the time. Mayall and the Bluesbreakers' version is as good as any with a passable, though unnecessary, drum solo by Hughie Flint. Listen to Eric launch into The Beatles 'Day Tripper' riff after emerging out of Flint's solo.

KEY TO LOVE
(Mayall)

A STANDARD R&B number driven by Eric's rhythm work and a horn section. His solo is short but intense and further proof, if any was needed, that he was the finest blues player in London at the time.

PARCHMAN FARM
(Allison)

THERE IS a certain piquancy in middle-class English chaps launching into the tearful lament of black inmates at one of the most notorious prisons in the Southern – and racist – American state of Tennessee. What could they know of the misery of the chain gang? The Bluesbreakers' version is led by Mayall on harmonica with no real involvement by Eric.

HAVE YOU HEARD
(Mayall)

STARTS slow and moody with some fine interplay between the horns and guitar, backed by the immortal sound of the Hammond organ. Eric's solo comes in 3.25 minutes into the song and is delivered as though his very life depended on it. Without doubt, one of the best solos he ever committed to tape; absolutely devastating, in fact, and reason enough to own this album.

Doubtless it was tracks like this that forced Mayall to add 'With Eric Clapton' to the title; apart from the commercial sense, Eric really was the star of the show.

RAMBLIN' ON MY MIND
(Trad.arr. Mayall)

ANOTHER live favourite with Eric that made regular appearances at concerts throughout the Seventies and Eighties. This was Eric's first lead vocal in the studio and he made sure that the others in the band had gone home before he recorded several takes. He needn't have worried as he comes over as totally confident. Keen listeners can even hear him tap his foot along to the beat.

STEPPIN' OUT
(Bracken)

A BLISTERING instrumental led by Eric's Les Paul, backed by a full horn section. Yet another opportunity for him to demonstrate his ample virtuosity at such an early stage in his career. This number was later to become his solo showpiece in concert during his time with Cream.

IT AIN'T RIGHT
(Jacobs)

AVERAGE boogie style number featuring Eric on rhythm guitar only and no solo.

PART THREE
CREAM

ERIC SOON TIRED OF SIMPLY COPYING HIS BLUES HEROES IN JOHN Mayall's band, and felt it was time to turn his artistry into creativity. He also recognised a kindred spirit in Jack Bruce.

Jack Bruce's bass style veered more towards jazz improvisation than blues and had proved a real eye opener for Eric, who was still playing note-perfect copies of Freddie King or Otis Rush solos. Having graduated from the Graham Bond Organisation to the Bluesbreakers, Bruce had opted out to briefly join Manfred Mann, principally for the financial rewards, but he soon tired of the pop world. He and Eric pooled their talents and recruited on drums Jack's former nemesis, Ginger Baker, another alumni of the Graham Bond Organisation with whom he had never really seen eye-to-eye. It was a volatile mix but for the time being the three virtuosi bottled up their emotions and rehearsed together in north London.

Sessions for their first recordings took place at Chalk Farm Studios and Mayfair Studios, London under the production aegis of manager Robert Stigwood. Curiously (and perhaps by band choice), the twee single 'Wrapping Paper' was left off the album, though its B-side, 'Cat's Squirrel' was included.

WRAPPING PAPER
Reaction 591 007;
released October 1966
(Bruce, Brown)

THIS RATHER strange vaudevillian number became Cream's first single, (released in October '66) and was written by Jack and his main songwriting partner, poet Pete Brown, whose association stretched back to jazz-poetry evenings with the Graham Bond Organization. It was hardly an auspicious début, and neither was it a true representation of their sound, especially as Eric plays only rhythm guitar throughout. In fact, to the best of the author's knowledge, Cream never played this song live. It reached number 34 in the UK charts.

CAT'S SQUIRREL
(Trad. arr. by S. Spurge)

THE B-SIDE was a harmonica and guitar based number with a short but superb lyrical solo by Eric.

Fresh Cream

Reaction 593001; released December 1966. CD: Polydor 5318102

I FEEL FREE
(Bruce, Brown)

LUCKILY FANS did not have to wait very long to hear Eric again. This was their second single, released on 9 December 1966, (the same day as *Fresh Cream*) and is an altogether better effort. Again written by Bruce & Brown, this up-tempo number demonstrated Eric's new found 'woman tone', a distinctive sustain technique he had developed in rehearsal. Great solo, great single, which reached number 11 in the charts in Jan' 67. In the Eighties, it was added to the CD version of the album as per the original US vinyl release.

N.S.U.
(Bruce)

WRITTEN by Jack Bruce, this 'driving' number was a great favourite in Cream's club shows and was later extended to a 15-minute epic on their arena dates in America. Eric produces a tight fluid solo. Despite the title there is nothing in the lyrics to suggest that the song is about a sexually transmitted disease!

As well as the lead-off track to the UK version of *Fresh Cream*, the song was released as the B-side to 'I Feel Free'.

SLEEPY TIME TIME
(Bruce, Godfrey)

WRITTEN by the songwriting team of Mr. and Mrs. Bruce, this slow blues-based song features a distinctive and sinuous solo by Eric. Another live favourite.

DREAMING
(Bruce)

THE SHORTEST song on the album, clocking in at just under two minutes. Very similar in style and feel to 'Wrapping Paper' and very dispensable with next to no guitar.

SWEET WINE
(Baker, Godfrey)

WRITTEN by Ginger and Jack's wife, Janet Godfrey, this is a highlight of the album which would become a long improvisational piece when performed live on their US tour of 1967. Eric plays double-tracked guitar solos throughout, producing a symphony of sounds unheard of at the time.

SPOONFUL
(Willie Dixon)

THE LONGEST track on the album and also a firm live favourite which became indelibly associated with Cream. Written by the late great Willie Dixon, Eric shows off a new maturity in his playing, experimenting with different guitars and amps to see what new sounds could be achieved. The studio version is every bit as good as the live versions, which could stretch up to 25 minutes.

CAT'S SQUIRREL
(Trad. arr. by S. Spurge)

AS DISCUSSED.

FOUR UNTIL LATE
(Trad. arr. Clapton)

WRITTEN by one of Eric's main influences, Robert Johnson. However, the adaptation here has none of Robert's angst and is performed more as a throwaway pop song.

ROLLIN' AND TUMBLIN'
(Muddy Waters)

JACK TOOK this fast-paced Muddy Waters tune and made it his own. A wild harmonica and guitar-led number that was a regular in their live set.

I'M SO GLAD
(Skip James)

ANOTHER blues original, this time written by Skip James. Eric made sure that Skip received all the royalty payments from 'I'm So Glad' which gave him a certain amount of comfort in his old age. Cream's version is a joyous up-tempo reading featuring a controlled, but nonetheless flamboyant, solo by Eric. When played live Eric would often throw in the lines to Tchaikovsky's '1812 Overture', as on the version recorded for the BBC in December 1966.

TOAD
(Baker)

GINGER'S *tour de force*, this instrumental gave ample opportunity for him to demonstrate his drumming ability in a long solo that would become even longer in the live concert arena. The sight of Ginger's limbs flying everywhere together with his fiery red locks was a wild sight, and must have been an inspiration for the mad drummer, Animal in *The Muppet Show*. Soon, many inferior bands in the rock field would subject their audiences to lengthy drum workouts.

THE COFFEE SONG
(Colton, Smith)

ATENTATIVE Cream in search of a style. This song remained unreleased in the UK until the Seventies when it was added as a bonus track to a reissue of the *Fresh Cream* album, but has been left off the current remastered CD.

Disraeli Gears

Reaction 593003; released November 1967

CREAM TOOK ADVANTAGE OF A SHORT VISIT TO AMERICA IN MARCH AND April 1967 to record their second album, *Disraeli Gears*, at New York's legendary Atlantic Studios under the production and engineering talents of Felix Pappalardi and Tom Dowd respectively.

This album – and the follow-up, *Wheels Of Fire*, which was conceived at the same time – represented Cream's important contribution to the so-called 'Summer of Love'. Eric, Jack and Ginger embraced psychedelia with no little enthusiasm; perming their hair, wearing colourful clothes and lapping up the almost obligatory mind expanding drugs. They also produced the best album of their career before the pressures of relentless touring extinguished the flame. *Disraeli Gears* was a groundbreaking effort and is one of the key albums that young musicians (particularly in America) often return to for inspiration from this golden era of exploration and creativity.

Tom Dowd, who also later worked with Eric in the Seventies and Eighties, recalls, "I remember Eric using a wah-wah and a pair of Marshalls turned all the way up. They recorded at ear shattering level."
The distinguished history of Atlantic's NY studios was not lost on Eric: artists such as Ray Charles, Aretha Franklin and Otis Redding had recorded there. For the sessions Eric had decided to use a Gibson SG, a small bodied cutaway guitar which had been customised in day-glo psychedelic colours by The Fool, a Dutch design team whose main customers were The Beatles. The tone of the guitar was not that different from the Les Paul he had previously favoured.

Jack had all of his songs ready for the album and as the band were playing live every day they were well-rehearsed. Eric had yet to assume complete confidence as a songwriter but he did co-write 'Tales Of Brave Ulysses', a third of 'Strange Brew' and contributed to a third of 'Sunshine Of Your Love'. At this stage he still preferred to arrange old blues numbers.

Eric laid down all his rhythm guitar parts first and later overdubbed his solos using several effects for the first time, including wah-wah pedals, fuzz tone and reverb. The result was a clear mixture of heavy blues and sparkling psychedelic guitar.

STRANGE BREW
(Clapton, Collins, Pappalardi)

CO-WRITTEN with producer Felix Pappalardi and his wife Gail Collins, Eric plays his best Albert King licks backed by some great Steve Cropper Stax-style rhythm work on the album's opening track. The song – a Cream classic – was also released before the album as a single in May 1967. Interestingly, another set of lyrics was also recorded using the same backing track. That number, titled 'Lawdy Mama', was later released on *Live Cream* and appears in two alternate versions on the expanded *Disraeli Gears* in 2004.

SUNSHINE OF YOUR LOVE
(Clapton, Bruce, Brown)

PERHAPS the best known Cream song of all. Jack Bruce's masterly ten-note bass riff – now permanently etched in the memory – opens a true rock classic which is still performed by Eric and Jack Bruce. At Cream's historic reunion concerts in 2005, it became the lone encore. Eric delivers a hard-edged solo, as well as occasional lead vocals. The studio version (released, due to popular demand, as a single in the US in February '68; in the UK seven months later) ends with jangling chords before fading out, whereas live it would give Eric an opportunity for another solo.

WORLD OF PAIN
(Collins, Pappalardi)

WRITTEN by producer Felix Pappalardi and his wife Gail, the lyrics tell a tale of a sad tree and a world of pain, backed by Eric's lilting wah-wah work and Ginger's hard hitting drum patterns. Eric recorded several overdubbed solos, giving the song a full rich sound.

DANCE THE NIGHT AWAY
(Collins, Pappalardi)

OPENING with a twelve-string Rickenbacker jangle that sounds for all the world as if Roger McGuinn had been brought in as second guitarist, this song is also written by the album's producer and his wife, and stands out from the rest of the album because of Eric's unique guitar sound. Never again in his entire catalogue would Eric adopt this style of 'Byrdsy'-playing.

BLUE CONDITION
(Baker)

TYPICALLY eccentric Ginger number featuring his unique 'talking' vocals with Eric providing only simple chord backing.

TALES OF BRAVE ULYSSES
(Clapton, Sharp)

A WAH-WAH pedal extravaganza about the wonders of the Greek Islands, this was written by

Eric and his then Chelsea flat-mate, Australian artist Martin Sharp, who also designed the album sleeve. Eric's wild wah-wah solo is another highlight of the album.

SWLABR
(Bruce, Brown)

FAST PACED Bruce/Brown composition with a typically nonsensical title and lyrics. The song title actually stood for 'She Walks Like A Bearded Rainbow' and features searing guitar work over some strong rhythm patterns.

WE'RE GOING WRONG
(Bruce)

ANOTHER classic Bruce number with a moody tone and somewhat prophetic lyrics. Eric offers a 'woman tone' solo over Ginger's tom-tom patterns and ends the song with a heavy barrage of 'Spoonful'-type riffs. The 'woman tone' was achieved by removing all the treble from the tone controls and either turning both pickups full on or simply using the rhythm pickup only.

OUTSIDE WOMAN BLUES
(Reynolds, arr. Clapton)

TYPICAL blues number arranged by Eric with psychedelic undertones throughout and a hard-edged *Bluesbreakers*-style solo. Eric also gets a rare opportunity to sing lead vocals. It was clear

how much more confident he was becoming as a singer but there is no doubt that Jack Bruce was the better singer of the two, and Eric was quite happy to leave the job to him.

TAKE IT BACK
(Bruce, Brown)

AN UNUSUALLY mundane blues number written by Jack Bruce and Pete Brown. Shuffles along nicely but Eric restricts himself mainly to rhythm work backed by rather strange party sounds throughout the track. Jack provides the harmonica solo where perhaps a guitar solo would have been more appropriate.

MOTHER'S LAMENT
(Trad. arr. Cream)

A FUN, BUT nevertheless throwaway, Cockney-style singalong that should have been relegated to a single B-side.

Disraeli Gears

(Deluxe Edition)

CD: Universal 9819312, released October 2004

THE CLASSIC **CREAM** ALBUM GETS THE **"DELUXE EDITION"** TREATMENT. Except for one track all this material has been previously available along with the BBC tracks. All are reviewed in this book. The new track is an alternate version of 'Blue Condition' with some Clapton vocals overdubbed. You also get both versions of 'Lawdy Mama' which were previously released on *Live Cream Vol. 1* and *Those Were The Days* box set respectively.

CD1 offers the stereo mixes of the original album, along with the alternate 'Blue Condition', 'Lawdy Mama' Version 2 (this is the version that was overdubbed to become 'Strange Brew') along with five demos that were previously released on *Those Were The Days*. CD2 has the mono mixes which had only been previously available on the now out-of-print DCC Gold Disc release. It also includes the alternate 'Blue Condition', 'Lawdy Mama' (Version 1) and nine BBC tracks. These are all taken from the 2003 *BBC Sessions* CD. This release offers the best sound so far for *Disraeli Gears*.

DISC 1: THE STEREO ALBUM (Tracks 1 – 11) plus 12. Lawdy Mama (Album Out-Take, Version 2) 13. Blue Condition (Previously Unreleased Alternate Version W/ Eric Clapton Lead Vocal) 14. We're Going Wrong (Demo) 15. Hey Now Princess (Demo) 16. Swlabr (Demo) 17. Weird Of Hermiston (Demo) 18. The Clearout (Demo)
(Tracks 12-18: all stereo)

DISC: 2 THE MONO ALBUM (Tracks 1 – 11) plus 12. Lawdy Mama (Album Out-Take, Version 1) 13. Blue Condition (Previously Unreleased Alternate Version, Eric Clapton Lead Vocal) 14. Strange Brew (BBC Recording) 15. Tales Of Brave Ulysses (BBC Recording) 16. We're Going Wrong (BBC Recording) 17. Born Under A Bad Sign (BBC Recording) 18. Outside Woman Blues (BBC Recording) 19. Take It Back (BBC Recording) 20. Politician (BBC Recording) 21. Swlabr (BBC Recording) 22. Steppin' Out (BBC Recording) (Tracks 12-22: all mono)

Wheels Of Fire

Polydor 583031; released August 1968 (July '68 in the US)
CD: Polydor 827578, October 1990

MOST OF THE *WHEELS OF FIRE* STUDIO ALBUM WAS WRITTEN AT THE same time as the previous album, *Disraeli Gears*. Recording started at IBC Studios, London in July 1967 and one of the first songs they laid backing tracks down to was 'White Room', another instant classic. Sessions were fitted in between tour dates and soon moved to Atlantic Studios in New York in September 1967 under the Pappalardi/Dowd team again. Considering they had to fly to New York from different parts of the US on their rare days off from touring, the album sounds remarkably fresh. The sessions continued spasmodically right through to June 1968, by which time the group were on the point of disbanding. By the end of the *Wheels Of Fire* sessions manager Robert Stigwood was reluctantly obliged to tell the world's press, "Cream are going to follow their individual musical policies."

The constant pressure of touring had gnawed away at whatever opportunities Cream had for creativity and as a result the atmosphere within the trio became unbearable. Never the best of pals, they now travelled to gigs in separate limos and at different times so as to avoid unnecessary personal contact with each other.

In between studio sessions, Cream also recorded several of their shows at Bill Graham's Winterland and Fillmore Auditorium venues for a live album to form a double album release with their studio tracks. Eric used a variety of guitars, Gibson SG, Gibson Firebird and Gibson Les Paul, throughout the album's four sides. Although Cream were disintegrating from the inside, *Wheels Of Fire* represented their most mature piece of work to date and one can only wonder what they could have gone on to create had they not been overworked and insensitively managed.

Disc 1 – In The Studio

WHITE ROOM
(Bruce, Brown)

AN EXPLOSIVE opener and a classic Cream number. Eric plays his solo like a man possessed, his frenzied wah-wah attack reaching devastating heights. Producer Felix Pappalardi played violas on the track which was also released as a single in October 1968 in the US; January '69 in the UK – months after the band had split.

SITTING ON TOP OF THE WORLD
(Burnett)

WRITTEN by Howlin' Wolf, Eric gets to play the role of Hubert Sumlin, Wolf's guitarist. Eric overdubbed some superbly fluid guitar runs over his grungy chord work. Not quite as frightening as the original, but nonetheless a great number which allows Eric to demonstrate his continuing maturity as a player together with his constant search to find new sounds.

PASSING THE TIME
(Baker, Taylor)

CO-WRITTEN by Ginger with British avant-garde musician Mike Taylor, known for his jazz instrumentation suites. Featuring Ginger on glockenspiel and Felix Pappalardi on organ pedals, the song starts fairly calmly before launching into a fast jam which on the original release faded out before seguing in to the delicate coda. However, when *Wheels Of Fire* was re-released in 1992 as a remastered gold compact disc edition, the complete unedited jam was intact.

AS YOU SAID
(Bruce, Brown)

SOMEWHAT surprisingly, Eric does not even feature on this track. Jack plays all the acoustic guitars, cello and vocal. Ginger contributes only the occasional hi-hat.

PRESSED RAT AND WARTHOG
(Baker, Taylor)

ANOTHER Ginger Baker co-composition with Mike Taylor, which features Felix Pappalardi on trumpet and tonette. Eric is initially fairly low in the mix under Ginger's nonsensical spoken lyrics. He gets to solo for a few seconds but is faded out just as he picks up momentum.

POLITICIAN
(Bruce, Brown)

A JACK BRUCE and Pete Brown classic featuring one of the

best bass guitar riffs Bruce ever wrote. Eric plays multi-tracked solos in unison to remarkable effect. A live favourite during their farewell tour.

THOSE WERE THE DAYS
(Baker, Taylor)

THE LAST of three Baker/Taylor compositions, this time featuring Felix Pappalardi on distinctive Swiss hand bells. Eric plays a wild solo.

BORN UNDER A BAD SIGN
(Jones, Bell)

BOOKER T. Jones, a.k.a. Booker T of The M.G.s, wrote this classic number which Albert King performed with his frightening guitar style. Eric certainly did the song justice, playing a hard edged solo which remains a highlight of the album.

DESERTED CITIES OF THE HEART
(Bruce, Brown)

ERIC PLAYS a frenzied out of phase double speed sitar-like sounding solo which suits the song's Far Eastern flavour rather well.

ANYONE FOR TENNIS
(Clapton, Sharp)

ERIC'S SOLE writing credit on the album, written originally for *Wheels Of Fire* (which it would not have sounded out of place on) but left off at the time, is a pleasant, rather whimsical, ditty which features Eric on acoustic guitar and overdubbed slide guitar on the outro. The only other instruments are congas, viola and mellotron. It was released as a single in May 1968 but only reached number 40 in the charts.

Disc 2 – Live At The Fillmore

CROSSROADS
(Johnson)

AT THEIR peak, Cream was a first class improvisatory unit and the second *Wheels Of Fire* disc was designed to highlight their mastery of the live medium. The live album kicks off with Eric in overdrive at Winterland in San Francisco on March 10, 1968, playing some of his most celebrated solos. The first is awesome and leaves you wondering just how he conjured up the sounds he did as well as where they came from. Just when you're about to recuperate, he hits you below the belt with another apocalyptic salvo. Eric still maintains he can't understand what all the fuss was about, which says a lot for his modesty.

There has been much speculation about the solo being cut to fit on the album, but the reality is quite different as this number was never one of their improvisatory pieces and there is no edit on the master tape.

SPOONFUL
(Dixon)

ALSO FROM Winterland on March 10, 'Spoonful' is the usual elongated extravaganza. Eric's solo takes us on a sixteen minutes-plus journey beyond the basic harmony and rhythmic chords of the original studio version. Here, he launches into manic freeform phrases behind Jack's pulsating bass runs and Ginger's forceful drum fills. It is not surprising that America held its arms open to Cream as true pioneers of a new age in improvisatory rock music.

TRAINTIME
(Bruce)

JACK'S SOLO piece recorded from Winterland on March 8. Eric usually slipped behind the amps for a quick fag during this number.

TOAD
(Baker)

GINGER'S solo piece, recorded at the San Francisco gig on March 8, took on a life of its own on stage. Eric solos along to Ginger's tom-tom patterns and double bass drum cannons before retiring from the fray, while Ginger lets rip for fourteen minutes plus.

Goodbye Cream

Polydor 583053; released March 1969. CD:Polydor 531815, April 1998

WHEELS OF FIRE **HAD GONE PLATINUM, SO IT SEEMED LIKE SOUND** marketing to try and repeat its success with another double album following the same format: a new studio album together with a live album recorded on Cream's farewell tour. Unfortunately, the band managed to record only three new studio tracks, one from each member, and the record company was left with no option but to release a single album instead.

Goodbye is a fitting epitaph, demonstrating how well the three performed together regardless of their disintegrating personal relationships. The studio material also offered a few clues as to what musical directions they would be aiming for as individuals.

Eric was hugely impressed by The Band's *Music From Big Pink* album and in particular he was drawn to the sound of Robbie Robertson's economic style of guitar playing. He also admired their versatility beyond the regular guitar, bass and drums rock band instrumentation.

On its release in March 1969, *Goodbye Cream* hit the Top 10 in both the UK and the US.

I'M SO GLAD
(James)

THIS (AND the following two tracks) were recorded on Cream's farewell tour of the US at the Los Angeles Forum on October 19, 1968. Played at breakneck speed, this live version is surprisingly together considering the personal animosities between band members. Eric plays like a demon, with some stunning backing from Jack and Ginger. When Cream were on this form no one could touch them, and this number is as clear an example of that as any currently available.

POLITICIAN
(Bruce, Brown)

STRONG and menacing version with Eric playing a sinuous solo. Listen out for his trademark vibrato halfway through.

SITTING ON TOP OF THE WORLD
(Burnett)

ERIC OBLITERATES the studio version with his playing: a flurry of crisp notes in the intro before a climactic solo which is without doubt his best solo on record since 'Have You Heard' from the

Bluesbreakers album.

On this form Eric's fluency was as magnificent as it was inexplicable, as if his fingers took on a life of their own which he was unable to control. Certainly, he was unable to explain it away, other than with a modest shrug.

BADGE
(Clapton, Harrison)

Recorded at IBC in London, 'Badge' is a Clapton/Cream classic which he has continued to perform live in concert throughout his career. Co-written with his friend George Harrison, who appears credited as L'Angelo Misterioso on rhythm guitar, Eric takes lead vocals and plays a short solo, but the most impressive part is the marvellous descending riff that rings out for the first time after the second verse and again later in the song.

Eric had the middle eight of the song ready, but little else, when he went over to George's house in Surrey. The song was completed in a day between the two of them, with a little help from Ringo who contributed the rather nonsensical line about swans living in a park and 'our kid' married to Mabel. The song was released as a single in April '69, reaching the UK Top 20.

DOING THAT SCRAPYARD THING
(Bruce, Brown)

JACK'S NUMBER is a disappointment and sounds as if it was written as a token gesture. Eric contributes only rhythm guitar played through a Leslie cabinet with a rotating paddle at the top to give the guitar a swirling Doppler effect normally associated with an electric organ. Eric later gave it to George Harrison who used it to great effect on The Beatles' classic 'Let It Be'.

WHAT A BRINGDOWN
(Baker)

GINGER'S number was perhaps the greatest surprise of the album in view of the random nature of his previous songwriting excursions. It's a mature piece which is arguably the best of the three studio numbers. Eric again plays through a Leslie but overdubs some great wah-wah licks. The track ends with Jack's fading organ... the end of Cream.

Live Cream

Polydor 2383016; released June 1970. CD:Polydor 531816, April 1998

CREAM MIGHT HAVE SPLIT UP BUT THAT DIDN'T NECESSARILY DIMINISH their earning potential, not from the record company's point of view at any rate. In the event, the marketplace would remain hungry for Cream for many years to come. The first post-Cream album was a 'Best Of' released in November 1968, the month of their two farewell concerts at London's Royal Albert Hall. A dull cover, inexplicably featuring coloured vegetables, coupled with the fact that no unreleased recordings were included contributed to poor sales.

Unfortunately there were no genuinely usable studio outtakes available, but many of their live shows had been recorded and this would prove to be a valuable and almost bottomless source of material. Two live albums were culled from shows at the Winterland and Fillmore venues in March 1968, as well as several numbers from their farewell tour in October 1968.

N.S.U.
(Bruce)

AN INSPIRED rendition of the Fresh Cream song, recorded at San Francisco's Winterland on March 10, 1968. This may have started life as a fairly simple pop song, but here it's transformed into a ten minute 'underground' epic. Ginger sets the pace with his distinctive drum opening followed by Eric and Jack's dual lead lines on guitar and bass. Eric's frantic soloing spits out lead lines seemingly out of nowhere, interspersed with menacing power chords.

SLEEPY TIME TIME
(Bruce, Godfrey)

ALSO FROM Winterland, this is longer than its studio counterpart, but the song remains the same. Eric's solo is longer and well constructed but surprisingly adds nothing to the original.

SWEET WINE
(Baker, Godfrey)

ANOTHER Winterland recording, this is without doubt the album's masterpiece with Cream at their live peak. Eric kicks in with his virtuoso solo after a minute's exceptional backing from Jack and Ginger. Short stabs, fluid bursts and stunning vibrato all go to make this fifteen minute piece a highlight of the entire Cream catalogue. It also acts as a perfect primer to the many different styles that Eric could incorporate within one song.

ROLLIN' AND TUMBLIN'
(Morganfield)

RECORDED at San Francisco's Fillmore Auditorium on March 7, 1968, this is a harmonica led Jack Bruce solo piece. Eric plays some wild licks in the left channel, and it's worthwhile turning the balance knob to the left just to hear Eric on his own. Marvellous stuff!

LAWDY MAMA
(Trad. arr. Clapton)

THE ONLY studio cut on this otherwise live album comes from the New York sessions at Atlantic Studios. This is the second version of 'Lawdy Mama', the first having been recorded during the *Fresh Cream* sessions. This was totally different in structure, with multi-tracked guitars, that was a live staple of the time. It's a shame that RSO decided to release this version, the less interesting, which is simply the backing track for 'Strange Brew' with the lyrics to 'Lawdy Mama'.

Live Cream Vol. 2

Polydor 2383119; released July 1972. CD:Polydor 531817, April 1998

DESERTED CITIES OF THE HEART
(Bruce, Brown)

A RARE LIVE outing of this *Wheels Of Fire* cut, recorded at Oakland Coliseum Arena on October 4, 1968, which is almost identical in structure to the studio original. Eric's solo is more traditional than the sonically embellished studio effort and the number lasts just over four minutes, which was short by their concert standards.

WHITE ROOM
(Bruce, Brown)

ALSO FROM the Oakland Coliseum show, this is a weak version that could never hope to overshadow the classic studio cut. Eric plays a suitably echoed wah- wah solo but the levels can be heard going up and down as the engineer tries to get the correct mix! Go back and listen to the *Wheels Of Fire* version.

POLITICIAN
(Bruce, Brown)

ANOTHER Oakland Coliseum track which fails to surpass the version from the LA Forum (released on *Goodbye*); it's nowhere near as menacing.

TALES OF BRAVE ULYSSES
(Clapton, Sharp)

A SURPRISINGLY good version from Winterland, with Eric in wah-wah overdrive.

SUNSHINE OF YOUR LOVE
(Bruce, Brown, Clapton)

'SUNSHINE' sounded more polished in a live context than in its studio version which, good as it was, gave the impression of finishing rather too abruptly. Here, Eric carries the song with gusto and playing with spirit right up to its natural conclusion. From Winterland.

STEPPIN' OUT
(Braken)

A CLASSIC piece of Clapton fretwork which was originally found on the *Bluesbreakers* album, and lasted only 2.26 minutes. At Winterland, Cream extended it into a 13.39 guitar extravaganza.

Cream
Those Were The Days

CD:Polydor/Universal 5390002, released September 1997

THE LAST WORD ON CREAM, FEATURING THEIR ENTIRE STUDIO OUTPUT along with many live tracks, some of which are unreleased. The set also has some fascinating demos from the *Disraeli Gears* sessions. The material unique to the box is as follows:

YOU MAKE ME FEEL
(Demo version)
(Bruce/Brown)

OUTTAKE from the *Fresh Cream* sessions. A more humourous side to the band.

WE'RE GOING WRONG
(Demo version)
(Bruce/Brown)

A REMARKABLY different version of this number. Eric and Jack using different chord progressions and sounding far more bluesy.

Eric Patrick Clapton, photographed in early 1965 around the time he left The Yardbirds to join John Mayall's Bluesbreakers. *(Harry Goodwin)*

The Yardbirds in 1964, left to right: Paul Samwell Smith, Chris Dreja, Keith Relf and Eric Clapton. Hidden behind them is drummer Jim McCarty. *(LFI)*

Five Live Yardbirds (1965)

Sonny Boy Williamson & The Yardbirds (1966)

The Yardbirds in 1964, left to right:
Paul Samwell Smith, Keith Relf, Jim
McCarty, Chris Dreja and Eric. (LFI)

Bluesbreakers With Eric Clapton
(1966)

The Bluesbreakers, left to right: John Mayall, Hughie Flint, Eric Clapton
and John McVie. *(Michael Ochs Archive/Redferns)*

Cream: Ginger Baker, Eric and Jack Bruce in late 1966. *(LFI)*

Fresh Cream (1966)

Disraeli Gears (1967)

Wheels Of Fire (1968)

Goodbye Cream (1969)

Ginger, Eric and Jack in 1967. *(LFI)*

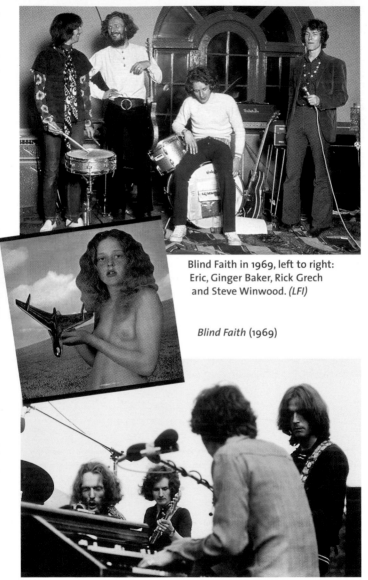

Blind Faith in 1969, left to right:
Eric, Ginger Baker, Rick Grech
and Steve Winwood. *(LFI)*

Blind Faith (1969)

Blind Faith in Hyde Park, London, June 7, 1969. *(Michael Putland/Retna)*

Eric collects his Melody Maker award as Best British Guitarist from John Peel, 1969. *(LFI)*

Layla And Other Assorted Love Songs (1970)

Derek And The Dominos: EC, Bobby Whitlock, Jim Gordon and Carl Radle. *(Michael Ochs Archive/Redferns)*

Eric on stage at the Hammersmith Odeon in 1974. *(LFI)*

The desolate finished take is far better. All in all a strong demo, finalised at Atlantic Studios.

HEY NOW PRINCESS
(Demo version)
(Bruce/Brown)

THIS IS A raucous Hendrix-inspired gem which includes some frantic instrumental work which has Jack's vocals struggling to keep up in parts. Eric produces an absolutely wild solo.

SWLABR
(Demo version)
(Bruce/Brown)

A GRITTY blues based version played at a slower tempo than the released version. Has some great playing by Eric.

WEIRD OF HERMISTON
(Demo version)
(Bruce/Brown)

UNFINISHED complex piece that would later be revisited by Jack on *Songs For A Tailor*. Eric follows Ginger closely while Jack emphasises the melody on bass. A shame they never finished this track; it would have been a great addition to *Disraeli Gears*.

THE CLEAROUT
(Demo version)
(Bruce)

GINGER'S drum rolls open this bizarre number. Jack's impro-

vised vocal melody of non-sensical lyrics has been wiped on this version. Eric just follows with some chord progressions, but it never leads anywhere. Sounds like a Who outtake.

FALSTAFF BEER COMMERCIAL
(Baker, Clapton, Bruce)

INTERESTING little ditty, based on the 'Sunshine Of Your Love' riff, recorded for Falstaff Beer to promote their product.

N.S.U.
[Live]
(Bruce)

PREVIOUSLY unreleased and unedited version. Eric is in amazing form and this is clearly a far superior version to that originally found on *Live Cream*.

TOAD
[Live]
(Baker)

PREVIOUSLY unreleased version with extended drum solo. Ginger at his best.

SUNSHINE OF YOUR LOVE
[Live]
(Bruce,Brown,Clapton)

RARE LIVE version taken from a TV performance on *The Glen Campbell Goodtime Hour* show in 1968.

Cream BBC Sessions

CD:Polydor/Universal 760482, released April 2003

THE **BBC'S** RECORDING STUDIOS WERE PRIMITIVE IN THE SIXTIES. THEY used two-track machines which allowed one-track for basic recording and one for overdubs which were then mixed down to mono. It was common for bands to overdub at the time as a way of achieving some similarity to the studio version. Unfortunately, many of the Sixties 'Beeb' recordings were either wiped or lost.

Cream's *BBC Sessions* contains 22 live-in-the-studio performances by Eric Clapton, Ginger Baker and Jack Bruce. It contains renditions of then-current singles like 'I Feel Free' and 'Strange Brew' as well as previews of upcoming album tracks like 'Tales of Brave Ulysses', 'We're Going Wrong', 'Born Under A Bad Sign', 'Politician', and 'Sunshine of Your Love'. Also contained are concert favorites like 'Traintime', 'Steppin' Out', and 'Crossroads', all recorded between November 1966 and January 1968. You also get four short Clapton interview segments, as well as rare photos, session info and notes in the CD booklet.

SWEET WINE
(Baker, Godfrey)

RECORDED on November 8, 1966 for BBC Radio, *Saturday Club* at the BBC Studios, London. Broadcast date 11 November, 1966. Same arrangement as the version found on the *Fresh Cream* album, recorded live in the studio.

WRAPPING PAPER
(Bruce, Brown)

CREAM DOES music-hall kitsch with overdubbing of piano and vocals. Same recording details as 'Sweet Wine'.

ROLLIN' AND TUMBLIN'
(Morganfield)

RECORDED live in the studio with no overdubs. This number was originally thought to have been lost. Same recording details as 'Sweet Wine'.

STEPPIN' OUT
(Bracken)

ORIGINALLY recorded for John Mayall's *Bluesbreakers* album. This BBC version has a lead guitar overdub. The basic track was laid down with rhythm guitar. Same recording details as 'Sweet Wine'.

CROSSROADS
(Johnson)

RECORDED November 28, 1966 for BBC Radio's *Guitar Club* at BBC Studios, London. Previously uncirculated, even on bootleg. It also predates the released version.

CAT'S SQUIRREL
(Trad. arr. S. Spurge)

RECORDED December 9, 1966, BBC World Service, *Rhythm & Blues*, BBC Studios, London. It was broadcast on January 9, 1967. Features overdubbed harmonica and vocals.

TRAINTIME
(Bruce)

RECORDED live in the studio. Same details as 'Cat's Squirrel'.

I'M SO GLAD
(James)

FEATURES overdubbed vocals and Eric's trademark '1812 Overture' quote in the solo, as he frequently did at this time when performing it live. Same details as 'Cat's Squirrel'.

LAWDY MAMA
(Trad. arr. Clapton)

THIS IS the Junior Wells arrangement of the song and can also be found on Eric's *Crossroads* box set. Details are as 'Cat's Squirrel'.

I FEEL FREE
(Bruce, Brown)

RECORDED January 10, 1967 for BBC Radio's *Saturday Club* at BBC Studios, London. It was broadcast on January 14, 1967. It features overdubbed vocals, claps, lead guitar and guitar solo.

N.S.U.
(Bruce)

WILD VERSION originally found on *Fresh Cream*. Features overdubbed vocals. Same recording details as 'I Feel Free'.

FOUR UNTIL LATE
(Trad. arr. Clapton)

FEATURES overdubbed vocals and harmonica. Same recording details as 'I Feel Free'.

STRANGE BREW
(Clapton, Collins, Pappalardi)

RECORDED May 30, 1967, for BBC Radio's *Saturday Club* at BBC Studios, London. It was broadcast on June 3, 1967. This is stunning, and more enjoyable than the studio version. Features overdubbed lead guitar and vocals.

TALES OF BRAVE ULYSSES
(Clapton, Sharp)

OVERDUBBED vocals and guitar. Same recording details as 'Strange Brew'.

WE'RE GOING WRONG
(Bruce)

PROBABLY even better than the version found on *Disraeli Gears*. Eric plays a neat solo. Features overdubbed vocals.

BORN UNDER A BAD SIGN
(Jones, Bell)

A SOMEWHAT tentative version of the Albert King Stax classic. Recorded on October 24, 1967 for BBC Radio 1's *Top Gear* at BBC Studios, London. It was broadcast October 29, 1967. Features overdubbed vocals and lead guitar.

OUTSIDE WOMAN BLUES
(Reynolds, arr. Clapton)

FEATURES overdubbed lead guitar and vocals. Quite a forceful version and better than the original found on *Disraeli Gears*. Same details as 'Born Under A Bad Sign'.

TAKE IT BACK
(Bruce, Brown)

SAME arrangement as the original version from *Disraeli Gears*. Features overdubbed harmonica, vocals & lead guitar. Same recording details as 'Born Under A Bad Sign'.

SUNSHINE OF YOUR LOVE
(Bruce, Brown, Clapton)

FEATURES overdubbed guitar solo which includes 'Blue Moon' quote. Same recording details as 'Born Under A Bad Sign'.

POLITICIAN
(Bruce, Brown)

RECORDED on January 9, 1968 for BBC Radio 1's *Top Gear* at BBC Studios, London. It was broadcast January 14, 1968. Features overdubbed vocals & lead guitar. Interesting, if tentative, version.

SWLABR
(Bruce, Brown)

FEATURES overdubbed vocals & guitar solo. Same recording details as 'Politician'.

STEPPIN' OUT
(Braken)

A LIVE FAVOURITE from the early days. This version is different in that each member has a lead break. Same recording details as 'Politician'. This version can also be found on the *Crossroads* box set.

PART FOUR
BLIND FAITH

AFTER **CREAM DISBANDED ERIC DECIDED TO REST AND TAKE STOCK** at the ample home he had bought in rural Surrey from the proceeds of the trio's high earning American tours. His liking for The Band's *Big Pink*, together with the nagging thought that Cream's live sound would have been improved with the addition of a keyboard player, led him to invite Stevie Winwood over for some informal jamming. Eventually, Ginger Baker was invited to join in. Eric wasn't so sure this was such a good idea as it felt as if his recent past was coming back to haunt him, but he decided to go with the flow. More formal sessions took place at Morgan Studios in February under the original name of Clapton, Baker & Winwood.

It wasn't long before management became involved and the term 'Supergroup' was bandied about in the press. Rick Grech, formerly with Family, joined the line up a month later as a multi-instrumentalist – like Winwood – and turned out to be a great asset to the band. Before they knew it they had an album deal and a huge American tour booked. Despite all Eric's wishes to the contrary, the pressure was on.

The sessions for the album were clearly just rehearsals, and producer Jimmy Miller was called in to salvage what he could and make an album out of it. The band didn't even have a name. With all the hype surrounding them, they rather cynically called themselves Blind Faith.

The resulting album, however, does hold a few surprises and is worth having in your collection, even though Eric's guitar is largely understated.

Blind Faith

Polydor 583059; released August 1969

HAD TO CRY TODAY
(Winwood)

A TYPICALLY wistful Winwood number that could have been recorded by Traffic. Stevie handles the vocals, as he does throughout the album, while Eric contributes an economical solo in the middle and Jimmy Miller has fun with the faders.

CAN'T FIND MY WAY HOME
(Winwood)

THIS BEAUTIFUL, haunting ballad is one of Stevie Winwood's best ever compositions and it has continued to feature regularly in Clapton's concerts throughout the years, even though it would be sung by a band member since Eric did not have the appropriate vocal range. Eric plays acoustic guitar accompaniment. An equally good electric version was also recorded and was first made available on Stevie Winwood's retrospective box set.

WELL ALL RIGHT
(Petty, Holly, Allison, Mauldin)

IT WAS SAID that Blind Faith wanted to record a whole album of Buddy Holly tunes. The truth is up for conjecture, but their shuffle version of 'Well All Right' is certainly more than passable. Eric plays rhythm guitar.

PRESENCE OF THE LORD
(Clapton)

THE VAGUELY mystical quality that surrounds Eric Clapton's life and work is best exemplified in ballads like this. 'Presence Of The Lord', Eric's best song from the Blind Faith era, manages to combine a religious intensity with an evocation of humility, as if he was seeking forgiveness for having risen above the commonplace. He wants Him to know that he didn't ask to be called God by his disciples.

'Presence Of The Lord' also features his best solo on the album, an expressive wah-wah flurry of emotion that was truly heartfelt.

Eric: "I wrote 'Presence Of The Lord' in C, which is pretty high for me. Also, I was very overwhelmed by Steve's presence as a singer. I don't think I could have stood out in the studio and sung it while he was there. I was totally without confidence at the time as a singer. That song was a true statement of what was happening in my life at the time. I had somewhere to live. I was actually having a good time after leaving Cream, feeling very secure. I was in a great frame of mind.

"That was just a song of gratitude. I'm not a religious person, never have been. But I've always found it very easy to say thank you to God, or whatever you choose to call Him, for whatever happens, which is nice to me. It's no problem for me to be grateful."

SEA OF JOY
(Winwood)

AGAIN, ERIC is relegated to playing acoustic accompaniment along with occasional electric licks on a meandering Winwood piece. Rick Grech is the main soloist, providing a haunting violin solo.

DO WHAT YOU LIKE
(Baker)

GINGER'S number sounded like a studio jam – the band glide along nicely as they find a groove – and a jolly good excuse for a solo. Eric offers an almost Santana-esque solo that shines with its economical beauty which is followed by the obligatory (and overlong) drum solo. The number ends in absolute mayhem when the band, as the track's title suggests, do what they like, offering further evidence that the track was largely unrehearsed.

Blind Faith
(Deluxe Edition)

CD: Polydor/Universal 314 542 529-2, January 2001

A DELUXE GATEFOLD 2-CD PACKAGE IN THE SAME SERIES OF UNIVERSAL'S "deluxe editions" that produced Cream's *Disraeli Gears* (see separate entry). As well as the original six-track album, the first CD also features 'Sleeping In The Ground' 'Can't Find My Way Home' (electric version) (both first released on the *Crossroads* box set – see entry – but here in new mix form), 'Acoustic Jam' , featuring Steve Winwood on piano and Eric on acoustic guitar, (plus bass and drums), 'Time Winds' – an unfinished song without a vocal, and 'Sleeping In The Ground' (Slow Blues Version). The second CD consisted of four jams – variously labeled: very long, good, and slow – each averaging out at 15 minutes, all taped on March 2, 1969, before Rick Grech joined the band. One of these jams became the foundation for the 'Change Of Address' single, which Island Records put out in the form of a "We've moved" notification. Blind Faith were originally going to be on Island, but ended up on Polydor (Atlantic in the U.S). The original master tape for the 'Change Of Address' jam is thought lost so the cut was dubbed from a mint condition copy of the original single – a rare collectors' item.

PART FIVE
THE SOLO YEARS
Eric Clapton

Polydor Super 3383021; released August 1970
CD: Polydor 5318192, August 1996

BLIND FAITH FIZZLED OUT RATHER THAN FORMALLY BROKE UP. NO official statement was made but Eric made up his mind to record a solo album and forget about the Blind Faith experience altogether.

One of the bands who had supported Blind Faith on their US tour was Delaney & Bonnie and Friends, a loose aggregation of friendly, laid back American session players who'd impressed Eric sufficiently for him to record some songs with them in Los Angeles during a break in the touring schedule. In return Delaney Bramlett agreed to produce his first solo album. In fact he was so impressed with the team that he brought them over to Europe for a short tour on which he (and, occasionally, George Harrison) joined them as a sideman. An album was recorded at Croydon's Fairfield Hall but it's hardly essential listening for fans of Eric's guitar playing.

Sessions for his first solo album began in England in November 1969 at Olympic Studios, Barnes. When Delaney & Bonnie returned to the States, so did Eric, and sessions moved to Village Recorders in Los Angeles. Delaney & Bonnie and Friends backed Eric throughout, and they invited other musicians – Steve Stills and Leon Russell among them – to join in.

Although the album appeared under the title of *Eric Clapton*, Delaney Bramlett's identity was firmly etched into its funky, white soul groove. Eric didn't seem to mind, though. Delaney had given him the confidence to sing and write more songs, and this confidence finally enabled Eric to change direction once and for all.

Eric: "In a way it (the album) was a vehicle for Delaney's frustrations with himself. He may have been projecting himself on me a lot. And that comes across a lot on the record. I don't mind it at all. I enjoyed it and learned a lot in the process. He was prepared to be my coach, and no one had ever offered that to me before. He was the first person to instill in me a sense of purpose. And he was very serious about it. He was a very religious person, saying things like 'You've got a gift. If you don't use it, God will take it away.' It was quite frightening when I looked at it that way."

An important factor in his new sound was the use of a Fender Stratocaster instead of his usual harsher Gibson arsenal. He also changed his amplification, from Marshall to Fender. And so began Eric's long love affair with American equipment and musicians, an apt compliment to their musical heritage.

SLUNKY
(Bramlett, Clapton)

STARTING life as a jam in the studio with Leon Russell, Bobby Keyes leads off with his inimitable sax playing before Eric cuts in with a rocking solo backed by the solid rhythm section of Carl Radle on bass and Jim Gordon on drums. Eric's echo-drenched cascades burst forth from his Fender Stratocaster at a relentless pace and amply display his new found sound. Sadly, it was a sound that alienated a blinkered fanbase who simply wanted to hear heavy Cream riffs played at notch 10 on a Gibson.

BAD BOY
(Bramlett, Clapton)

A WAH-WAH based number that rocks along nicely and features a fluid solo by Eric.

LONESOME AND A LONG WAY FROM HOME
(Bramlett, Russell)

WRITTEN by Delaney Bramlett and Leon Russell, Eric first heard this number during a Bramlett-produced King Curtis session and decided to record it himself after hearing that Curtis didn't like his singing on the track. Again, Eric uses wah-wah in a subtle way, as in Motown's session ace 'Wah Wah Watson's' style which embellished rather than overpowered the song.

AFTER MIDNIGHT
(Cale)

J.J. CALE'S sparse, shuffling guitar style, and soft, haunting vocals were the epitome of the laid-back sound that found a distinctive niche in rock during the early Seventies. It appealed to Eric, as did Cale's modesty – he shunned the limelight despite his popularity – and Eric must often have wished that he too could conjure up a similar low profile.

This number became a firm

favourite with Eric throughout the Seventies. It always cooked, and Eric plays only a short solo which allows him to concentrate on his vocals. By now, with a little help from peppermint schnapps, he'd found his own vocal style which he put to good use throughout the whole album.

EASY NOW
(Clapton)

AN UNDERRATED love song, composed by Eric and performed as a solo piece with simple guitar accompaniment. In this writer's opinion, 'Easy Now' is far more sincere than the syrupy but far better known 'Wonderful Tonight' which was written six years later. Eric obviously disagrees, since he performed the number on only a handful of occasions on his 1974 US tour.

BLUES POWER
(Clapton, Russell)

NOW A classic rock number that Eric played live throughout the Seventies and Eighties. After a deceptively quiet intro the drums kick in with such a staggering force that the listener is almost knocked back into his seat.

BOTTLE OF RED WINE
(Bramlett, Clapton)

NICE SHUFFLE with appropriate solo. Written on the way to

the studio on a day when neither Eric nor Delaney had prepared any songs to record.

LOVIN' YOU, LOVIN' ME
(Bramlett, Clapton)

PROBABLY the weakest song on the album. Ironically, this was originally written for Blind Faith, but Eric changed it around slightly to suit his vocal style rather than Steve Winwood's, and recorded it for this album.

TOLD YOU FOR THE LAST TIME
(Bramlett, Cropper)

WITH M.G.'s guitarist Steve Cropper on board for the session it's no surprise that this track has a strong Stax feel. No solo, but exemplary rhythm work and vocals make this track enjoyable.

DON'T KNOW WHY
(Bramlett, Clapton)

A SUPERB gospel feel with Eric's most emotive vocals on the album, backed with simple fluid guitar runs throughout. Written in England at Eric's and performed on the Delaney & Bonnie tour in December 1969.

LET IT RAIN
(Bramlett, Clapton)

ANOTHER highlight and eventual Clapton classic which Eric

has now performed in concert almost as many times as 'Layla' and justifiably so. An epic number with a strong vocal performance and the album's best guitar solo, which again showed off his new-found affinity with the Fender Stratocaster.

'Let It Rain' became a concert favourite throughout the Seventies and Eighties, retaining the same arrangement and similarly structured solo. Several live versions with different bands are available.

Layla And Other Assorted Love Songs

Polydor Super 2625005; released December 1970

AFTER THE SESSIONS FOR *ERIC CLAPTON* WERE OVER ERIC RETURNED home to plan his next move – the album that is now widely regarded as the finest work of his career.

He had enjoyed working with the American musicians a great deal and was keen to form a band and hit the road. Luckily for him he was able to secure the services of Bobby Whitlock, Carl Radle and Jim Gordon, all of whom had left Delaney & Bonnie's Friends and were seeking berths elsewhere.

Rehearsals began at Eric's Surrey home and the team also cut their teeth at the sessions for George Harrison's stunning *All Things Must Pass* album at London's Abbey Road. This was an ironic twist of fate as Eric's biggest influence for his next album was actually Pattie Boyd, George's wife, with whom he had fallen hopelessly in love. This as yet unrequited affair would inspire the wonderful music he was soon to record but there was a downside too: it also hurled him headfirst into an addiction to heroin and alcohol that would take years to finally absolve.

The songs he wrote and the cover versions he chose to record on *Layla And Other Assorted Love Songs* were all subliminal messages to Pattie, perhaps none more so than 'Have You Ever Loved A Woman?' with its stark references to adultery with the 'woman who bears another man's name'. Hindsight simplifies this analysis, but there can be little doubt now that Eric's *Layla* LP is perhaps the greatest and most emotional love letter ever recorded by a rock musician.

The sessions for *Layla* took place at Miami's Criteria Studios under the production talents of Tom Dowd. Shortly after the start of recording, Duane Allman, at that time the finest slide player in America, was asked to join and on top of everything else the double album remains a fine testament to two guitarists at their peak, having a ball playing together.

Masterful, emotive, gargantuan, epic, heartfelt... all these epithets apply to this all-time classic album. If Eric had never played another note, *Layla And Other Assorted Love Songs* would have assured him an honourable mention in any rock history.

I LOOKED AWAY
(Clapton, Whitlock)

WEARING his heart on his sleeve, Eric opens with a beautiful love ballad, as sad as it is innocent. With vocals shared between Eric and keyboard player Bobby Whitlock and a deceptively simple solo by Eric, 'I Looked Away' sets the romantic tone for all that will follow. It is backed with a solid rhythm section that most bands would die for, the crucial factor that prevents the album's message from dragging or becoming self-absorbed.

BELL BOTTOM BLUES
(Clapton)

ANOTHER hauntingly romantic song that is now a cult favourite amongst dedicated Clapton fans. Rarely played live, Eric throws in some delicate chime-like harmonics before settling into a solo of such sensitivity that it makes you weep. His singing admirably complements his playing.

KEEP ON GROWING
(Clapton, Whitlock)

ERIC CHOPS his way into a song highlighted by lush textured layers of intertwined guitars reminiscent of the Delaney & Bonnie sound.

NOBODY KNOWS YOU WHEN YOU'RE DOWN AND OUT
(Cox)

BACK TO Eric's first love, the blues. Duane plays delicate slide fills beside Eric's plaintive vocals. Bobby Whitlock provides some suitably bluesy Hammond sounds before Eric offers up a throaty solo on his trusty Strat.

I AM YOURS
(Clapton, Nizami)

A BEAUTIFUL Eastern flavoured tabla drum driven song with lyrics taken directly from Ganjavi Nizami's love poem, *The Story of Layla and Majnun*. Eric related heavily to the book which inspired the title track of this album.

ANYDAY
(Clapton, Whitlock)

A STRONG self-assured number which again features rich textured layers of guitars over which Eric and Bobby Whitlock sing in unison about lost love.

KEY TO THE HIGHWAY
(Segar, Broonzy)

L IVE AND without overdubs, 'Key To The Highway' is a fine example of Eric and Duane having fun with a blues jam. Their interplay is dynamic and unselfish, each giving the other plenty of space in which to stretch out. Eric's vocals are authentic in feel, but take second place to his fluid and intense solos. A fair amount of the album came out of jams such as this with Tom Dowd rolling the tapes pretty much constantly. This is why the song fades in.

TELL THE TRUTH
(Clapton, Whitlock)

'T ELL THE Truth' was originally recorded with Phil Spector during the sessions for George Harrison's *All Things Must Pass* triple set, but discarded by Eric who was dissatisfied with Spector's production. Re-recorded in Miami with Tom Dowd at the controls, this version satisfied Eric.

It was played at a much slower pace than the frantic original, with Eric and Duane both playing slide guitar to great effect and Jim Gordon and Carl Radle keeping the backing solid as they do throughout the album.

WHY DOES LOVE GOT TO BE SO SAD?
(Clapton, Whitlock)

F AST GUITAR lead number whose title summed up Eric's feelings very succinctly. His playing is incendiary – as though he were exorcising some demon from his soul.

HAVE YOU EVER LOVED A WOMAN?
(Myles)

T HE AUTOBIOGRAPHICAL quotient on this emotional blues song seemed almost too perfect for a man who'd fallen for the wife of his best friend. Perhaps the ultimate Clapton vehicle for sheer intensity, the emotion he displays in his playing is even rawer here than in 'Layla' itself. Putting every bit of himself into the song, he almost throttles the neck of his Strat, squeezing everything possible from wood and steel. Stunning, and the real highlight of the album.

LITTLE WING
(Hendrix)

ERIC HAD been in awe of Jimi Hendrix's playing ever since they met shortly after Jimi arrived in London in 1966. Hendrix jammed with Cream that same year and both players enjoyed a mutual respect – Eric even perming his hair in an effort to emulate Jimi. 'Little Wing' first appeared on *Axis: Bold As Love* and is one of Jimi's most lyrical ballads.

Eric actually recorded the song in Miami just two weeks before Jimi died in London and, heartbroken when he heard the news, decided to retain his own haunting version on the album as a tribute to his friend.

IT'S TOO LATE
(Willis)

BACK TO the blues with a typical theme of lost love. Duane slides and Eric sings.

LAYLA
(Clapton, Gordon)

ALTHOUGH not the foundation on which the Clapton legend was built, 'Layla' is certainly the pillar which kept it strong for two decades. It is unquestionably Eric's best-known song, a tearful plea to his girl Layla – or Pattie as the case might have been – to take heed of his unrequited love. Certainly, it burns with fierce intensity, helped by Duane's screeching slide work, before mellowing out into Bobby Whitlock's piano lament which is intercrossed with Eric and Duane's weeping guitars. Although it's a truly beautiful piece, it has become an albatross around Eric's neck as he is now expected to play it at every concert, and it suffers through over-familiarity as a result.

'Layla' became a hit single in the summer of 1972, almost two years after this album was released, and again in 1982.

Eric: "I had no idea what 'Layla' was going to be. It was just a ditty. When you get near to the end of it, that's when your enthusiasm starts building, and you know you've got something really powerful. You can be so-so as you're making the track, singing the vocals, but if as you start to add stuff and mix it, it becomes gross, then you really are in charge of something powerful. What I'm saying is, when I started to do that, it didn't feel like anything special to me. If you try to write something that's already got all of that, it's impossible. You just try to write something that's pleasing, and then try to get it to that.

"I'm incredibly proud of 'Layla'. To have ownership of something that powerful is something I'll never be able to get used to. It still knocks me out when I play it. You know what? That riff is a direct lift from an

Albert King song. It's a song off the *Born Under A Bad Sign* album ('As The Years Go Passing By'). It goes 'There is nothing I can do/If you leave me here to cry'. It's a slow blues. We took that line and speeded it up.

"But the funny thing was that once I'd got 'Layla' out of my system, I didn't want to do any more with The Dominos. I didn't want to play another note. I went back home and stayed there and locked all the doors."

THORN TREE IN THE GARDEN
(Whitlock)

AFTER THE storm, the album signs off with a gentle acoustic love song from Bobby Whitlock.

Layla

20th Anniversary Edition

CD Polydor box set 5318202; released December 1990

A BEAUTIFULLY REMASTERED VERSION OF THE *LAYLA* ALBUM WAS RELEASED in a special three CD box set in 1990 to celebrate its twentieth anniversary. The double album now fitted nicely onto a single disc, with two further discs of unreleased outtakes and jams from the original sessions. The package also included copies of the original studio session sheets.

Disc 1 – Layla

TRACK LISTING AS ABOVE.

Disc 2 – The Jams

JAMS 1 – 5

OF INTEREST TO DIEHARD FANS ONLY. THESE JAMS DEMONSTRATE CLEARLY how well this unit gelled together and, of course, feature extended solos by Eric and Duane Allman that are particularly enlightening since they reveal how the sessions developed. Sadly, most buyers will probably content themselves with Disc 1.

Disc 3

HAVE YOU EVER LOVED A WOMAN?
(Alternate Master 1)

A GOOD alternative version with a great guitar solo, but overall this lacks the intensity of the previously released version.

HAVE YOU EVER LOVED A WOMAN?
(Alternate Master 2)

YET ANOTHER version, featuring some inspired playing during Eric's solo but, again, failing to surpass the original.

TELL THE TRUTH
(Jam 1)

PREVIOUSLY available only on the Polydor double album *History Of Eric Clapton*. An interesting jam without Duane but plenty of licks by Eric.

TELL THE TRUTH
(Jam 2)

THIS SECOND jam is looser and lengthier than the first but still lacks inspiration although there is enough interesting playing from

Eric to make it worthwhile listening. Just as you think the jam ends, Jim Gordon suddenly picks up the tempo and increases the pace, followed by the others with Eric playing different styles and throwing in the odd Chuck Berry lick here and there. If nothing else, the jam shows a band that at this stage were so tight it seems they could do no wrong.

MEAN OLD WORLD
(Rehearsal)

GREAT BLUES number that never made it on to the final album in its rehearsal stage. Loose, but interesting.

MEAN OLD WORLD
(Band Version – Master Take)

FINISHED version featuring Eric and Duane on guitars and Jim Gordon on bass drum. Another song about problematic love.

MEAN OLD WORLD
(Duet Version – Master Take)

PREVIOUSLY available on a Duane Allman compilation, this version differs greatly from the band version. It's clear that Duane and Eric had much in common musically, and it must have been a tough decision for Duane to return to his own band after these sessions.

IT HURTS ME TOO
(Jam)

UNSPECTACULAR version of the Elmore James song.

TENDER LOVE
(Incomplete master)

AVERAGE rehearsal for a never completed number. Mildly interesting at best.

IT'S TOO LATE
(Alternate Master)

GOOD alternate version.

Derek And The Dominos In Concert

RSO 2659020; Released March 1973. CD: Polydor October 1990

DEREK AND THE DOMINOS BEGAN TOURING IN AUGUST OF 1970 before they'd even started recording *Layla And Other Assorted Love Songs*, and they went straight back on the road when it was completed. Their touring (in the US and UK) continued until the end of the year but in May 1971 they disbanded over disagreements during the recording of their second album. Drugs undoubtedly played a significant role in the band's disintegration.

RSO never wasted an opportunity to make money out of Eric, so it came as no surprise that several shows were recorded for later release, including four New York concerts at the famous Fillmore East in October 1970, all of which were introduced by the late Bill Graham.

WHY DOES LOVE GOT TO BE SO SAD?
(Clapton, Whitlock)

AFUNKY intro jam leads into this excellent live version. Eric soars on his Fender Strat with strong backing from his Dominos.

GOT TO GET BETTER IN A LITTLE WHILE
(Clapton)

ANOTHER funky jam type song that was unrecorded at the time they performed it live, this was often used as an opener to give The Dominos an opportunity to whip up a nice groove. Eric opens the throttle and wails away to his and the audience's evident satisfaction.

LET IT RAIN
(Clapton, Bramlett)

A LENGTHY version of the track which originally appeared on his solo album and which was played by almost every band Eric led, this was a truly classic Clapton song that takes on epic proportions in the live forum. Jim Gordon really swings on this outing, demonstrating what an excellent drummer he was at the time. Eric solos at length but, as throughout the album, it is obvious that without a foil of Duane Allman's stature to play against, he finds it hard to find inspiration.

PRESENCE OF THE LORD
(Clapton)

T HE INTRO receives rapturous applause from the New York crowd as do Eric's appropriately tortured vocals. His wah-wah solo at 2.30 into the song is heartfelt.

TELL THE TRUTH
(Clapton, Whitlock)

A N IDEAL number for jamming which, unfortunately in this instance, seems to go nowhere. Eric and the band sound tired and uninspired.

BOTTLE OF RED WINE
(Clapton, Bramlett)

G OOD SHUFFLE from his first solo album. The 23rd October night was clearly the better show with Eric and his Dominos sounding as though they're actually having fun. Great solo by Eric and tight drums from Jim Gordon.

RSO should have had the balls to release the whole gig, warts an' all, as it was truly a memorable show.

ROLL IT OVER
(Clapton, Bramlett)

O RIGINALLY found on the flip side of their quickly deleted Phil Spector-produced début single, 'Tell The Truth'. Wah-wah led number that would not have sounded out of place on Eric's first solo album. Exceptional solo by Eric makes this one of the album's highlights.

BLUES POWER
(Clapton, Russell)

G REAT LIVE vehicle for Eric on this quasi-autobiographical number. Eric visits every fret on his guitar and plays a storm. Superior to the original studio version.

HAVE YOU EVER LOVED A WOMAN?
(Myles)

PERFORMED as though his very life depended on it, Eric's sinuous intro shone through the darkened Fillmore East with just his shadow against the red lights of his Fender amps. As he approached the mike a single spotlight revealed the emotional angst in his face. He stepped back from the mike into the darkened stage at 4.37 into the song and ripped out a solo that only a man with a broken heart could play. The obvious but definite highlight on this album.

Derek And The Dominos Live At The Fillmore

CD : Polydor 521682; released February 1994

POLYGRAM RE-RELEASED THIS ALBUM IN 1994 AS PART OF THEIR 'Chronicles' reissue program. Seven previously unissued tracks graced the new updated version which was now also remastered.

FULL TRACK LISTING: Got To Get Better In A Little While/Why Does Love Got To Be So Sad?/Key To The Highway/Blues Power/Have You Ever Loved A Woman?/Bottle Of Red Wine/Tell The Truth/Nobody Knows You When You're Down And Out/Roll It Over/Presence Of The Lord/Little Wing/Let It Rain/Crossroads

The previously unreleased numbers are as follows:

WHY DOES LOVE GOT TO BE SO SAD
(Clapton, Russell)

BETTER version from the magical 23rd October show. Much more frantic, Eric kicks the wah-wah pedal with venom in the lengthy intro passage. His searing solo is so much better that it makes you wonder who was responsible for selecting the tracks for the original project, as they must have had cotton wool in their ears!

KEY TO THE HIGHWAY
(Segar, Broonzy)

THE SLEEVE erroneously lists the recording date as 24th October, it is actually from the previous night. Good live rendition, but adds nothing to the already excellent 'live in the studio' version from the *Layla* album.

TELL THE TRUTH
(Clapton, Whitlock)

A MORE exploratory version than previously released. Eric slips on his slide for his solo, taking the listener to previously uncharted territory.

NOBODY KNOWS YOU WHEN YOU'RE DOWN AND OUT
(Cox)

FAITHFUL version of Jimmie Cox's 'Nobody Knows You When You're Down And Out,' which was originally recorded during the *Layla* sessions.

LITTLE WING
(Jimi Hendrix)

THIS VERSION of 'Little Wing' was previously available only as a free flexi disc with the May 1988 issue of the US magazine *Guitar Player*. It was also issued as a limited promotional issue coupled with a remixed studio version for the release of the 20th Anniversary *Layla* box set. A faithful live rendition where Eric has to work even more than usual as Bobby Whitlock's organ inexplicably breaks down halfway through the number.

LET IT RAIN
(Clapton, Bramlett)

A MAGNIFICENT epic 18.19 minute version that outshines the previously released version from the following night. It opens with Whitlock's wailing organ, which had failed halfway through the previous number, 'Little Wing', but was now in full flight. Eric's playing far outshines the previously released version and listen out for some inspiring 'call and answer' between Eric and Jim Gordon halfway through the drum solo.

CROSSROADS
(Johnson)

ENCORE time sees a welcome return of Robert Johnson's 'Crossroads', albeit at a much slower pace than the version on Cream's *Wheels Of Fire* album. Stunning solos by Eric, including a telling change of lyric about going back to Ewhurst, his home village.

Eric Clapton's
Rainbow Concert

RSO 2394116; released September 1973
CD: Polydor 527472, July 1995

ERIC'S SELF-IMPOSED HIBERNATION INTO A WORLD OF DRUGS BETWEEN 1970 and early 1974 is well documented in many biographies. Obviously, nothing much was heard from him musically during this period, but he was tempted out of his home by his friend Pete Townshend for a one-off show at Finsbury Park's Rainbow Theatre on Saturday, January 13, 1973. In fact, he played two concerts that night, early evening and late evening, and both were recorded by Who soundman Bob Pridden on the Ronnie Lane Mobile which was parked behind the venue.

Eric almost didn't make the first show, having discovered at the last moment that the trousers on the suit he intended to wear were far too tight owing to his bad dietary habits. His girlfriend Alice Ormsby-Gore was summoned to let them out which delayed Eric's arrival at the Rainbow by several hours. Meanwhile Townshend et al bit their fingers. Eric actually arrived ten minutes before curtain-up, with the audience in their seats and completely unaware of the dramas that had occurred backstage.

Backed by his friends – Townshend, Stevie Winwood, Rick Grech, Ronnie Wood and Jim Capaldi – Eric was in surprisingly good form but the resulting album really did not do the shows justice. Bad mixing and poor production effectively eliminated any subtleties of the playing.

Eric: "I thought the gig was OK. I had a good time doing it. It was when I listened to the tapes afterwards that I realised that it was well under par. It was like a charity benefit in a way, you know. They got me out, got me on stage and tried to get me at it and I was being pushed more than I was pulling. I did it really because it was for Pete most of all. I wasn't really ready to go on stage. Although my reluctance was great I really loved the feeling. The welcome I got really moved me, it really did.

"I think there were too many people on stage for the way it was recorded. They recorded it on something like an eight track and so they had to mix a lot of things together while they were recording, which meant that the rhythm section suffered and you got the bass and drums mixed in together. It was just not very satisfactory in that aspect. I mean, it was very hard to mix."

BADGE
(Clapton, Harrison)

CHAOTIC version with Pete Townshend's characteristic, Who-style crashing chords everywhere in the mix. Eric offers a good solo, however, but a bad edit at the end of the song somehow prepares the listener for further disappointments in store.

ROLL IT OVER
(Clapton, Whitlock)

NEVER the most spectacular stage number, this live outing gives the band an opportunity to jam along nicely but without direction.

PRESENCE OF THE LORD
(Clapton)

STEVIE Winwood sings and plays the keyboard intro to one of Eric's finest songs. Eric kicks in at 3.06 minutes with an inimitable wah-wah solo backed by Pete's usual powerful chord work. Ronnie Wood is largely lost deep in the mix, which is a shame as he played superbly throughout in his role of rhythm guitarist.

PEARLY QUEEN
(Winwood, Capaldi)

OBLIGATORY Traffic number played with conviction and style by all concerned. An echoey mix with heavy emphasis on Jim Capaldi's cymbals ruins the recording. The three guitarists provide some tight chord work and Eric plays his best Dave Mason solo.

AFTER MIDNIGHT
(Cale)

GOOD LIVE rendition of J.J. Cale's 'After Midnight,' which was originally recorded for Eric's first solo album. Eric and Ronnie provide solos.

LITTLE WING
(Hendrix)

CHAOTIC, but heartfelt version dedicated to their friend Jimi Hendrix.

461 Ocean Boulevard

RSO 2479118; released August 1974 CD: Polydor 5318212, August 1996

APART FROM AN APPEARANCE AT GEORGE HARRISON'S CONCERT FOR Bangla Desh in August of 1971, Eric spent almost three years locked away dealing with his personal problems. With Pattie now at his side, he announced his return to the music scene in April 1974, and booked studio time at Miami's Criteria Studios in sunny Florida while his old cohort from the Dominos, bassist Carl Radle, recruited a band for the sessions.

Now more than ever Eric was determined to distance himself from the guitar god tag that had become an albatross around his neck. To that end very few solos graced his new album, *461 Ocean Boulevard*, but – paradoxically – it was to prove one of his most popular ever. Soon after its release Eric and his band undertook a massive tour of America, performing before hundreds of thousands of fans at giant arenas. Often they were supported by The Band.

Eric's new band now comprised Carl Radle on bass, Jamie Oldaker on drums, Dick Sims on keyboards, George Terry on second guitar, and Yvonne Elliman, who had made her name in *Jesus Christ Superstar*, on extra vocals.

Eric: "I really had no ideas for *461* before I went to Miami. I just jammed and put it together as I went along. I played everything I could think of. I must have gone through a hundred songs. But I was frightened to expose myself to too much by bringing out the stuff I had written on my own during the three years before. I didn't really know anyone in the band. So we all just wrote there, or made things up. I left the tapes with Tom Dowd and said, 'Pick out what you think is best and put it on the album'."

MOTHERLESS CHILDREN
(Trad. arr Clapton)

A SPECTACULAR feast of overdubbed guitars opened this funky number. Carl Radle had assembled a tight unit who had played together in Tulsa backing Bob Seger, amongst many others. In George Terry, Eric again found a perfect foil who inspired him to spectacular heights, particularly in concert. Eric plays some superb slide using an open A tuning. Extended outros were also the norm!

WILLIE AND THE HAND JIVE
(Otis)

JOHNNY Otis' choppy classic is given the EC treatment and became a live staple during his tours in 1974. The band sound really together and Eric's vocals had clearly matured, with fluctuations and intonations that were convincing rather than tentative as in the past. In fact on these sessions he appeared to put more effort into his singing than his guitar playing.

GET READY
(Clapton, Elliman)

A PERFECT follow-up to 'Willie', this slow sexy number became another live favourite. Eric and Yvonne Elliman deliver their steamy song with great passion.

I SHOT THE SHERIFF
(Marley)

BY COVERING Bob Marley's 'I Shot The Sheriff' and turning it into a US number one hit single, Eric effectively popularised reggae music, and Bob Marley, its principal figure, in particular. This was no mean feat as America had hitherto largely ignored the subtle rhythms emanating from just south of Florida.

The original master tape shows that the actual recording was much longer and included a guitar solo. Here, the long introduction is missing, with the number starting straight in and fading out at the end.

Eric: "George Terry played me the *Burnin'* album, by Bob Marley & The Wailers, that had 'I Shot The Sheriff' on it. It took me a while to get into it. I was coming from a completely different place. To break my inherent musical tightness down into this real loose thing was very, very difficult for me to assimilate.

"The 'Sheriff' track was conceived in Miami, with a Tulsa band. It was such a weird melting pot. The only way I could stamp my personality onto it was to sing it, and just play the occasional lick. The rest of it was almost out of control. It was a complete hybrid.

"The record came out, and went up the charts, and shortly after that I got a phone call from Bob Marley. I don't remember where I was, or exactly what the circumstances were, but we had a half-an-hour conversation on the phone. And I kept asking him if it was a true story – did he really shoot the sheriff? What was it all about?

"He wouldn't really commit himself. He said some parts of it were true, but he wasn't gonna say which parts. The next time I spoke to him, he came to England with The Wailers and did a small tour – until one of them got sick with 'flu. None of them had ever had the 'flu before. They thought he had a serious disease. They cancelled the tour and went home, 'cause it was cold then in England. But I went to see them at the Hammersmith Odeon, and I walked into the dressing room that I couldn't see the other side of because of the smoke. I sat and talked to Bob, and he was just a great guy. He was so warm. A beautiful man. This was our first face-to-face meeting."

I CAN'T HOLD OUT
(James, arr. Clapton)

A WONDERFUL version that oozes feeling whilst Eric's slide solo in an open E tuning drips with raw emotion. His vocals are another highlight, expressing a newfound warmth.

PLEASE BE WITH ME
(Boyer)

C HARLES Scott Boyer was in a great outfit called Cowboy who released several albums on the Capricorn label and became a firm favourite of Duane Allman. Eric plays a beautifully tender version of this song on acoustic. Again, his singing shows amazing versatility backed by his simple dobro embellishments.

LET IT GROW
(Eric Clapton)

H AUNTING ballad that showed Eric with his heart on his sleeve. The dobro and acoustic guitar accompaniment could not

have been further from Cream's raw intensity, as a result tracks like this alienated many former fans, but at the same time it brought Eric many new fans who were unaware of his past.

STEADY ROLLIN' MAN
(Johnson, arr. Clapton)

U PTEMPO version of this Robert Johnson number, with a short but enjoyable solo by Eric.

MAINLINE FLORIDA
(Terry)

W RITTEN by guitarist George Terry and sung by Eric, this uptempo song was probably the nearest to an all-out rock song on the entire album.

GIVE ME STRENGTH
(Clapton)

P ERHAPS the most sensitive dobro-led number on the record. Written towards the end of his heroin addiction, Eric pleads to *Him* for strength. Short but direct.

There's One
In Every Crowd

RSO 2479132; Released April 1975 CD: Polydor 5318222, August 1996

IN BETWEEN *461 OCEAN BOULEVARD* AND *THERE'S ONE IN EVERY CROWD*, Eric and his band played a huge US tour in 1974, and by the time they hit Dynamic Sound Studios in Jamaica they were gelling together perfectly as a unit. *There's One In Every Crowd* was clearly an attempt to carry on where the previous album had left off. Marcy Levy, now better known as Marcella Detroit of Shakespear's Sister, had been recruited to add extra harmony vocals.

As it was recorded in Jamaica, a reggae influence was more evident, although many other influences shone through as well. There's a gospel feel to many of the tracks, perhaps the result of the backing singers, and also a nod towards the country blues style of America's southern states.

The album's title came from one of Eric's favourite sayings at the time. This is a sadly overlooked album, which this author still insists is one of Eric's best.

Eric: "Tom got us there for *There's One In Every Crowd*, which was almost 50-50 reggae stuff and Marcy Levy songs. When we got there, people were just wandering in and out of the studio, lighting up these massive trumpet joints. After a while, I didn't know who was in the studio and who wasn't, there was so much smoke in the room."

WE'VE BEEN TOLD
(JESUS COMING SOON)
(Johnson, arr. Clapton)

PERHAPS more than any other of his albums, *There's One In Every Crowd* demonstrates Eric's increasing eclecticism. The wide variety of styles may not have been exactly what his fans wanted but Eric seemed determined never again to slot into a predictable bag. This song was gospel based, performed in a country blues style with Eric playing some tasty dobro licks. A stunning arrangement with full credit going to Marcy and Yvonne for inspired vocals.

SWING LOW SWEET CHARIOT
(Trad. arr. Clapton)

ANOTHER sympathetic arrangement by Eric. A heavily 'reggaefied' version, with Eric adopting Jamaican style vocals backed by the girls. Occasional slide guitar accompaniment rounds off a well-executed performance.

LITTLE RACHEL
(Byfield)

WRITTEN by 'Rockin' Jim Byfield who recorded on Leon Russell's Shelter label. A simple R&B tune with Eric clearly enjoying himself singing, but his guitar is a little too laid back.

DON'T BLAME ME
(Clapton, Terry)

WRITTEN as a sequel to 'I Shot The Sheriff', this reggae tinged number grooves along nicely with some great staccato riffs by Eric.

THE SKY IS CRYING
(James, Robinson)

ERIC CONTINUES his love affair with Elmore James with this fine version. Moody organ and keyboards back Eric's menacing slide work and emotive vocals.

SINGIN' THE BLUES
(McCreary)

WRITTEN by Leon Russell's wife Mary McCreary, who also recorded on Shelter, a favourite label with Eric for several years and a great source of reference. He even recorded several tracks with Mary which have yet to be released. Funky guitar chops and slide lines lead into the song, followed by the rest of the band. Eric plays a short solo.

BETTER MAKE IT THROUGH TODAY
(Clapton)

LAID BACK, intimate and warm. This is the album's highlight and one of Eric's best songs but it has sadly been overlooked due to the album's lack of chart success. His truly heartfelt lyrics are matched by a short but beautifully executed wah-wah tinged solo.

PRETTY BLUE EYES
(Clapton)

PLEASANT love song with beautiful Beatlesque harmonies which recall the suite of mostly Paul McCartney penned ballads on side two of Abbey Road. Eric contributes gut string acoustic guitar accompaniment and solo.

HIGH
(Clapton)

AN ACOUSTIC intro leads into a harmony drenched track that is also reminiscent of The Beatles. Eric comes in with electric during the outro. Interestingly, this number was first tried out during Derek and The Dominos' aborted second album sessions.

OPPOSITES
(Clapton)

A SWEET and sugary number, recorded at Criteria Sound Studios on their return from Jamaica. The lengthy outro passage features delicate playing between Eric and George Terry on slide. Again, beautiful harmonies indicate a clear Beatle influence with very Harrison-like slide guitar fills. Wonderful!

EC Was Here

RSO 2394160; released August 1975 CD: Polydor 5318232, August 1996

WHILE ERIC WAS FIGHTING TO RID HIS IMAGE AS A GUITAR HERO ON his studio albums, RSO became increasingly concerned about their lack of guitar solos. Several concerts were therefore recorded for a live album to feed a guitar-hungry public. However, just prior to the start of his huge 1975 USA tour, Eric and his band recorded two tracks for a one-off single, a cover of Bob Dylan's 'Knockin' On Heaven's Door' backed with 'Someone Like You' (released August 1975) but this recording is remembered more for the controversy surrounding its release rather than the tracks themselves.

Recently Eric had played on a session for Jamaican born Arthur Louis on which he actually laid down guitar parts for a version of 'Knockin' On Heaven's Door'. He liked it so much, he recorded his own version, using the same arrangement and an Arthur Louis original as the B-side to return the favour. Unfortunately, Arthur released his version a few weeks before Eric's, but he received hardly any airplay when faced with such auspicious competition. Nevertheless, Louis' cover version is worth seeking out.

RSO recorded several concerts in the US and in England during his 1974 and 1975 tours with a view to releasing a much-needed guitar based album. *EC Was Here* was the result. Throughout these tours Eric's

American band was on top form, a direct result of the almost constant live work, and the only criticism about the album is that it could, and should, have been a double.

Nevertheless Eric himself wasn't convinced about the wisdom of this release. "I didn't really want to put it out now," he said at the time. "But the record company was worried about the sales of *There's One In Every Crowd*. They thought if they put out a live record to coincide with a tour, that it would sell. I don't really understand their thinking, but I went along with them. I picked out the best tracks we had around. If there's any concept, it's an accident."

HAVE YOU EVER LOVED A WOMAN?
(Myles)

FROM LONG Beach Arena, Long Beach, California, July 19, 1974. An incredible opening gambit where Eric half sings the lyric and lets his guitar finish the remainder. Before you know it, George Terry and Eric are scraping each other off the ceiling with some particularly fierce guitar sparring. Fans who thought that Eric had given up on guitar solos could feel satisfied.

PRESENCE OF THE LORD
(Clapton)

RECORDED on the second of two nights at Long Beach Arena, Eric sings his most sacred song with powerful vocal accompaniment from Yvonne Elliman. Eric hits the pedal for a heavy solo that completely obliterates the original studio version, and Jamie Oldaker shows why he was the best drummer Eric ever had.

DRIFTING BLUES
(Moore/ Brown/Williams)

ALSO RECORDED at Long Beach on July 20, Eric returns to his only true love, the blues. There's an exciting acoustic guitar intro full of licks, vibrato and string bends that shows his virtuosity on that instrument before he switches halfway through to electric, causing rapturous applause from the crowd. A few tuning problems don't detract from his stunning, albeit wild, slide playing before suddenly changing key and launching into a slow 'Ramblin' On My Mind'. The CD version is the complete eleven minute version which was originally faded out after only a few minutes on the vinyl version.

CAN'T FIND MY WAY HOME
(Winwood)

A BEAUTIFUL version of Stevie Winwood's 'Can't Find My Way Home' sung by Yvonne Elliman with backing vocals from Eric who provides an exceptional acoustic solo. George Terry too is on fine form playing some stinging lead work. Also from the second Long Beach show.

ferent in construction to the previous version. Here the Gibson's dirty sound is more authentic than the thin Fender Strat sound.

RAMBLIN' ON MY MIND
(Johnson)

RECORDED at Hammersmith Odeon, London, on December 4, 1974, Eric whips out his Gibson Explorer for another version of 'Ramblin' On My Mind'. Sadly, the number has been edited, which means we are deprived of a stunning version of 'Have You Ever Loved A Woman?' which was performed halfway through the number in a different key. Eric's solo is exemplary and quite dif-

FURTHER ON UP THE ROAD
(Veasey/ Robey)

THE ONLY track from his 1975 tour (Nassau Coliseum, New York, June 28) is a driving blues number made popular by Bobby Bland, and Eric and his band stir it up in this hair-raising version. A live favourite throughout the years, Eric and George Terry let rip in a fashion not too dissimilar from the old Yardbirds 'rave ups'. The album finishes as it started, on a high.

No Reason To Cry

RSO 2394160; released August 1976
CD: Polydor 5318242, September 1996

THE *NO REASON TO CRY* SESSIONS TOOK PLACE AT THE BAND'S Shangri-La Studios in sunny Malibu, California, overlooking the Pacific. Many friends dropped by to jam and guest on the album, including Bob Dylan, The Band, Georgie Fame, and Ronnie Wood. The Band and Eric first jammed together in the basement of Big Pink, their communal Woodstock home, in 1968. Eric was totally smitten with their first album, *Music From Big Pink*, and this was a major factor in Cream's demise. Their pure Americana sound seemed so different from anything Eric had ever played before – and so intoxicating – that he felt his musical future lay in that style. However, it was not until 1976 that he actually had the opportunity to record with them.

The studio had once been a bordello and the main room was all wood and provided great acoustics. Due to a dispute between RSO and

Atlantic, Tom Dowd, who was Atlantic's in-house producer, was unable to work with Eric. The Band's soundman Ed Anderson engineered the early part of the sessions. Rob Fraboni came in towards the end of the recording to mix and produce the finished album.

Inevitably the influence of The Band can be heard throughout the album. Various Band members contributed songs, played and sang. His lengthy admiration for The Band undiminished, Eric was delighted to at last be playing and recording with them. The results, however, attracted criticism because Eric's personal signature seemed to have been lost amid the contributions from others.

BEAUTIFUL THING
(Manuel/Danko)

'BEAUTIFUL Thing' is a wonderful number written by The Band's Richard Manuel and Rick Danko that suits Eric's lilting style perfectly. Ronnie Wood is prominent on slide while Eric is content to play the role of backing musician, as he does throughout the album.

CARNIVAL
(Clapton)

A LATIN American number that was originally recorded with The Rolling Stones in a drunken overnight session at Electric Lady Studios in New York, but could not be used for contractual and alcoholic reasons! Re-recorded during the Malibu sessions, the number starts with Eric's cockney shout of "Oi!" before the whole band kick in with a relentless beat. All that's lacking is a much needed solo. The live version per-formed during the 1975 tour had a much better arrangement.

SIGN LANGUAGE
(Dylan)

A FINE DYLAN number taken as a duet between Bob and Eric. Robbie Robertson plays a series of tasty licks throughout while Eric again limits himself to dobro accompaniment.

COUNTY JAIL BLUES
(Fields/arr. Clapton)

ERIC SLIPS and slides his way through more familiar territo-ry on this blues tune. His growl-ing vocals were beginning to show the signs of too much smoking, but this lament suited his husky voice.

ALL OUR PAST TIMES
(Danko)

RONNIE Wood plays lead guitar while Eric sings plaintive vocals on this Rick Danko tune.

HELLO OLD FRIEND
(Clapton)

ERIC USED this number to open most of his 1976 concerts and it was obviously a favourite of his at the time. Simple acoustic strumming and pedal steel guitar are the predominant sounds in this country ballad.

DOUBLE TROUBLE
(Rush/arr. Clapton)

FOR MANY, this represented the album's highlight. Eric had always admitted that Otis Rush was a major influence and this is one of Rush's saddest numbers. Eric wails and sings his heart out while Dick Sims plays some moody organ fills. In the live forum, this song took on a life of its own and would often stretch to fifteen minutes of guitar heaven. However, back in the studio it still sounded mean and moody and features the only real solo guitar playing by Eric throughout the album.

INNOCENT TIMES
(Clapton/Levy)

JOINTLY written with Marcy Levy, who sings lead, this is a light country ballad. Eric plays exquisite dobro, as he always does when he plays that instrument. When's the solo dobro album, Eric?

HUNGRY
(Simms/Levy)

AN INDIFFERENT song that has a fairly catchy line but seems to go nowhere, simply plodding along with no apparent involvement from Eric, save for some tasty slide licks.

BLACK SUMMER RAIN
(Clapton)

ANOTHER gem, this little known song by Eric has a beautiful melody and sweet lyrics. Simple in structure but sincere in execution with a trademark solo and anguished vocals.

LAST NIGHT
(Clapton)

BONUS TRACK, available only on CD, recorded during Eric's infamous 31st birthday party session where the tapes were left rolling. Recorded live, it sounds that all concerned were having a good time, but it was a case of "you had to be there."

Slowhand

RSO 2479201; released November 1977
CD: Polydor 5318252, September 1996

ERIC AND HIS BAND RECORDED *SLOWHAND* IN **MAY 1977** AT **OLYMPIC** Studios in Barnes, the first time Eric had used a British studio since the aborted second album by Derek & The Dominos.

The sessions were produced by Glyn Johns, one of Britain's most experienced producers who'd worked with The Beatles, The Rolling Stones, The Who, The Eagles and many more top names. Somewhat of a martinet, Johns did not take kindly to Eric's drunken antics and many arguments ensued as the sessions progressed.

Nevertheless, the resulting album was a huge success and provided Eric with some of his greatest hits, including his most successful romantic ballad 'Wonderful Tonight', the rollicking 'Lay Down Sally' and the crowd pleaser 'Cocaine' whose riff sounded almost identical to Cream's 'Sunshine Of Your Love'.

Eric's influences were now extending to Don Williams and John Martyn, as well as old favourite J. J. Cale, and at times it was difficult to recognise this album as the work of the intense blues guitarist who'd inspired fans to daub 'Clapton Is God' on London's masonry.

Eric: "*Slowhand* for me is a very nervously sung album, especially after *No Reason To Cry*. Maybe it was because of the lack of material we had when we went in to cut it, or the difference in surroundings.

"And laid back is not the word for it! *Layla* wasn't a success, it died a death, but as far as I was concerned, I'd have put that album up against anybody's that was out at the time. With *Slowhand* it was a completely different story. It was lightweight, really lightweight, and the reason for that, I think, is partly due to the fact that some of the stuff that we wanted to put on the record I wrote, say, six months before. We were on the road and we wrote some songs and got to the studio – and we couldn't get the studio early enough or we wanted a couple of weeks off or something like that – and by the time we got in there everyone knew the song so well, we were so sort of limp about it that it was lazy."

COCAINE
(Cale)

J. J. CALE was an influence on Eric since he first heard 'After Midnight'. He took 'Cocaine', added a measure of rhythmic bite and made it his own, and it became one of his most requested songs to play on stage. Eric plays a great solo on faithful 'Blackie'.

WONDERFUL TONIGHT
(Clapton)

ERIC'S BEST known romantic ballad has probably been played at more weddings throughout the world than any other song, barring Mendelssohn and Wagner's Wedding Marches.

Noodling around on a handy acoustic during an interminable wait for Pattie to select an outfit for a party they were attending that evening, Eric came up with the entire song. He can't have had any idea what impact Pattie's dressing routine would have over the years: couples young and old have doubtless proposed, made or declared love while it's been playing.

Eric: "I think the best track has got to be 'Wonderful Tonight', because the song is nice. It was written about my sweetheart, and whether or not it was recorded well or we played it well doesn't make any difference, because the song is still nice.

"Every now and then you fall in love again, albeit with the same woman, just one night for some reason – something she's said or the way she's approached the situation, and bang, you're in love again, and it's such a strong feeling you can't do anything else but write it down."

It's a far cry from the blues but still a classic in the Clapton songwriting canon.

Widely believed also to have been the inspiration behind 'Something', first husband George Harrison's most admired Beatles love song, not to mention Eric's 'Layla', Pattie Boyd can lay claim to being one of the 20th century's most effective muses for songwriters in romantic mode.

LAY DOWN SALLY
(Clapton/Levy/Terry)

AND THE hits keep coming! Another smash and firm stage favourite that topped the US country charts. Eric plays some tasty licks in a clearly J. J. Cale-influenced shuffle number.

NEXT TIME YOU SEE HER
(Clapton)

ERIC GOES country again with a nod to Don Williams. Simple changes and a lightweight solo by Eric.

WE'RE ALL THE WAY
(Williams)

A FAITHFUL cover that suits Eric's voice admirably. For many, however, this was too much country and not enough Eric.

THE CORE
(Clapton)

A GREAT recurrent riff makes this one of the album's highlights. Marcy's vocals are excellent and Eric solos like a demon. Mel Collins on sax is a pleasant surprise as the two intertwine in a rising crescendo of notes. The whole band cooks on this one.

MAY YOU NEVER
(Martyn)

AFTER THE storm, the calm. A pleasant cover of John Martyn's 'May You Never' again shows which direction Eric's music would be heading in over the next few years. Eric plays an acoustic guitar for accompaniment.

MEAN OLD FRISCO
(Crudup)

A RTHUR Crudup is perhaps best known for writing 'That's All Right?', the first commercially released recording by Elvis Presley. Another tune first tried out during the aborted sessions for Derek & The Dominos' second album. Eric plays some dirty slide and appropriate growling vocals.

PEACHES AND DIESEL
(Clapton/Galuten)

A FINE instrumental that sounds similar to 'Black Summer Rain' from No Reason To Cry. Obviously a love song that should have had lyrics. If it had it might well have been as popular as 'Wonderful Tonight'. Eric plays an echoey solo that suits the mood admirably.

Backless

RSO 2479221; released November 1978
CD: Polydor 5318262, September 1996

TRYING TO RECAPTURE THE SUCCESS OF *SLOWHAND*, ERIC RETURNED TO Olympic and Glyn Johns but they were unable to conjure up the same brew of commercial tracks and crowd pleasers as they had a year earlier.

Perhaps the worst problem was that Eric's American band had become stale and a terminal apathy seemed to have set in. They'd now been playing with Eric for almost five years, and although Eric had paid them well, certain members of the outfit had gambled away their earnings which led to ill-feeling and a certain desperation. There is no doubt that their minds were not always on the job.

Coupled with this was the nagging realisation that the material they recorded lacked the quality of the songs Eric had written or selected the previous year.

Similar in tone, *Slowhand* and *Backless* could have been combined to make a compatible double set but there is no question that *Backless* was the weaker of the two. Eric seemed to realise this, albeit belatedly, and he fired the band within months of its release. Their fate was cast to the wind: Carl Radle, who'd been the band's musical director, died in the early Eighties of a drug overdose; keyboard player Dick Sims ended up working in a factory; George Terry and Jamie Oldaker returned to session work. Only Marcella Detroit, now Marcy Levy, seemed to have benefited from five years as a member of Clapton's band – later joining up with ex-Bananarama singer Siobhan Fahey in the '80s duo, Shakespear's Sister.

WALK OUT IN THE RAIN
(Dylan/Springs)

ONE OF two songs, co-written with Helena Springs, that Bob Dylan gave Eric to record. "He laid this cassette tape on me," Eric later said. "I've still got it. That's another bootleg. When I get down sometimes, I listen to them and it will bring me right out. This is a gift to me."

Eric and his band chug along nicely enough, but in hindsight the song is no great shakes.

WATCH OUT FOR LUCY
(Clapton)

GOOD shuffle in a similar vein to 'Bottle Of Red Wine'. Eric rocks along nicely to this pleasant little ditty.

I'LL MAKE LOVE TO YOU ANYTIME
(Cale)

ANOTHER J. J. Cale cover where Eric adopts Cale's vocal style and lilting wah-wah backing to stunning effect. It was a firm favourite on EC's 1978 European tour where the number was extended for some inspired jamming.

ROLL IT
(Clapton/Levy)

THIS SOUNDS like it started life as a jam on a repetitive riff which forms the basis of this number. Its only redeeming factor is some fine slide playing by Eric. Marcy sings the simple lyrics.

TELL ME THAT YOU LOVE ME
(Clapton)

AN UNSURPRISING Clapton original that was still very much in a country mould. Good guitar fills throughout but Eric's vocals are unconvincing.

IF I DON'T BE THERE BY MORNING
(Dylan/Springs)

THE SECOND of the two Dylan numbers. More uptempo than 'Walk Out In The Rain' as well as being more poppy in sound. The band sound sluggish though, but Eric puts in a nice solo on faithful 'Blackie'. The song was played live quite frequently during the 1978 and 1979 tours.

EARLY IN THE MORNING
(Trad. arr. Clapton)

THIS IS more like it. Eric's heart was still in the blues even though he was sounding more Don Williams than Muddy Waters. This number restores faith with its sleazy slide patterns played over a basic blues workout. The CD version has the previously unreleased full version which had previously faded out on the original vinyl album. Listen to Eric's gruff vocals and exquisite slide solo as well as Marcy's fine harmonica playing. A treat!

PROMISES
(Feldman/Linn)

BACK INTO country territory for a track that reached the US top ten. Don Williams must have been proud. The only redeeming factor in a song that was an inferior re-write on the melody of 'Lay Down Sally' is Eric's fine dobro playing in the background.

GOLDEN RING
(Clapton)

ERIC'S FEELINGS at the time sum up this number and the rest of the album pretty succinctly, "I got away with one song on there, 'Golden Ring', which I think is the strongest song on the album, because I was fed up with the general apathy of everyone involved." 'Golden Ring' is indeed a fine song and certainly representative of the album, but whether you feel it is the strongest is purely down to personal taste.

TULSA TIME
(Flowers)

WRITTEN by Don Williams' guitar player, Danny Flowers, Eric and his band seem to at last liven up with this slide driven number that became a firm live favourite for many years.

Just One Night

RSO 2479240; released May 1980
CD: Polydor 5318272, September 1996

WITH THE AMERICAN BAND DISPERSED, AN ALL-ENGLISH BAND WAS hired in its place. Guitarist Albert Lee was a session veteran and without doubt the finest country style guitar player Britain has ever produced; as affable as he was talented, Lee's past credits included working with Joe Cocker, The Everly Brothers and Emmylou Harris. Keyboard player Chris Stainton had made his name with Joe Cocker as a member of the original Grease Band, and the rhythm section, bassist Dave Markee and drummer Henry Spinetti, were equally experienced.

The problem with this UK band, however, was that they were unable to jam quite so readily as the Americans. They were certainly exceptional musicians, but they hadn't grown up amid the improvisatory feel that so many American rock musicians take for granted. As a result, the arrangements of Eric's songs on *Just One Night* lacked the ingredients of previous albums and often sounded regimented and cold as a result.

The new band's first appearance on record was this live album recorded at Tokyo's acoustically perfect Budokan in December 1979. Although worth having in your collection, it certainly does not represent Eric at his live best. Sadly such an album has yet to be released.

Eric: "I didn't really want to record it. There's a natural shyness about me when I'm playing on stage; for me it's something that should only happen once, you know, and then it's gone. The album was one show. We did it two nights, and recorded both. I think they chose the one I didn't like."

TULSA TIME
(Flowers)

THE LOYAL Japanese fans applaud enthusiastically as Chris Stainton plays some teasing piano as an introduction to a rollicking live version of 'Tulsa Time'. His new English band turn in a superior version to the studio counterpart. Eric plays some fancy slide work which glides nicely into the next number.

EARLY IN THE MORNING
(Trad. arr. Clapton)

THE RHYTHM section don't seem to be able to play the blues as well as their American counterparts, but Eric more than compensates with some emotive vocals and searing slide guitar work which was played on a sunburst Fender Stratocaster.

LAY DOWN SALLY
(Levy/Terry/Clapton)

A FAITHFUL reproduction, complete with good solo, of the great crowd pleaser.

WONDERFUL TONIGHT
(Clapton)

A NOTHER faithful copy. It would take several years and bands to change the arrangement in concert.

IF I DON'T BE THERE BY MORNING
(Dylan/Springs)

A LIVELY rendition of Bob Dylan's number from *Backless*. Eric and Albert Lee share vocal duties. Albert plays one of his trademark guitar solos and Chris Stainton plays a piano solo. A criticism of Eric at this time was that he would often devote too much time to other members of his band.

WORRIED LIFE BLUES
(Merriweather)

M UDDY Waters used to love hearing Eric perform this number. Eric obviously enjoyed singing and playing it too. Keyboard solos are followed by an expressive volley of searing licks by Eric.

ALL OUR PAST TIMES
(Clapton/Danko)

THE *No Reason To Cry* chestnut was occasionally played in concert and, judging by the applause, it was certainly a favourite among Japanese fans. Surprisingly, its transition to the live setting works well with Albert taking over Rick Danko's vocals and Eric playing a sensitive solo to match.

AFTER MIDNIGHT
(Cale)

A NOTHER live staple of the time, this rendition is performed at breakneck speed and features a fiery wah-wah solo by Eric. A definite highlight on this double album.

DOUBLE TROUBLE
(Rush)

E RIC IS always at his best when playing the blues. This is no exception. He sings his heart out to a background of buzzing amps and seemingly effortless licks. The song builds in tempo until Eric lashes out with a menacing solo before bringing the tempo back down to a low down and dirty finish in a crescendo of licks. Classic!

SETTING ME UP
(Knopfler)

ALBERT Lee's solo spot on a song by Dire Straits' Mark Knopfler.

BLUES POWER
(Clapton/Russell)

ALWAYS a live favourite with Eric and fans alike, this number cooks with a vengeance. Albert's lilting piano intro quickly lets way to a fast paced version which is counted in by Eric. He rips out a lengthy wah-wah solo driven by Albert's piano, Henry Spinetti's drumming and Dave Markee's bass runs.

RAMBLIN' ON MY MIND/HAVE YOU EVER LOVED A WOMAN?
(Myles, arr. Clapton)

ANOTHER blues classic giving Eric ample opportunity to shine. Originally recorded with John Mayall's Bluesbreakers, Eric revisits his roots. His vocals have clearly matured since those days. He keeps the band on their toes by calling out key changes halfway through soloing and playing a storming 'Have You Ever Loved A Woman?'.

COCAINE
(Cale)

A CONCERT favourite for many years which usually signalled the crowd to advance to the front of the stage. As the first few chords are played the audience predictably goes wild as Eric and crew put in a memorable performance. Eric again hits the wah-wah pedal for a lengthy solo which he almost loses control of halfway through.

FURTHER ON UP THE ROAD
(Veasey/Robey)

A FITTING encore to a good show. This uptempo number would also introduce the band before starting into the song itself. Not as good as the other live version found on *EC Was Here*.

Another Ticket

RSO 2479285; released February 1981
CD Polydor 5318282, September 1996

ERIC FELT THE NEW BAND NEEDED SOME GUIDANCE TO HELP THEM LOOSEN up and to that end he took on as unofficial musical director his friend Gary Brooker, formerly the leader of Procol Harum, and before that, The Paramounts, whom Eric knew from his Yardbirds days. Initial sessions for their first studio album with Eric started at Surrey Sound in England under the supervision of Glyn Johns, but it quickly became apparent that things were not going well, and the sessions came to an abrupt halt in a frenzy of accusatory arguments.

One problem was that Eric's record company discovered that Albert Lee and Gary Brooker were recording their own songs, or at least taking too great a role in the proceedings to the detriment of Eric's own ideas and direction, and felt this was not in Eric's or their own best interests.

The sessions were moved to Nassau with a new producer, Eric's old sparring partner Tom Dowd, with whom he last worked on *461 Ocean Boulevard*. The band was retained but their opinions weren't sought, and the resulting album, *Another Ticket*, turned out to be a bluesy affair but despite the record company's role in the proceedings it was largely over-looked due to lack of promotion.

When the new band went out on tour to promote it, Eric managed to play only a handful of gigs in the US before collapsing on stage and being rushed to hospital with an ulcer ready to burst. He was off the road long enough to damage sales, which is a great pity as *Another Ticket* is a very good album.

Another Ticket showed off Eric's new maturity as a songwriter, and incorporated more guitar than the previous three studio albums. It seemed that perhaps he'd learned to live with the fact that people wanted his guitar regardless of his own feelings, so this time around he might as well give them it; maybe he'd finally exorcised the gnawing resentment at the attitudes that drove him to minimise his guitar play-ing on his earlier solo records.

SOMETHING SPECIAL
(Clapton)

ERIC PLAYS some lilting licks over his vocals. Gary Brooker's influence can clearly be heard on this and most of the album.

BLACK ROSE
(Seals/Setser)

NICE SLIDE work opens this largely country number. Eric's vocals are exceptional as indeed they are throughout the album, showing the whole gamut of his range.

BLOW WIND BLOW
(Waters)

GREAT rendition of Muddy's 'Blow Wind Blow' which made a welcome reappearance at Eric's blues concerts at the Royal Albert Hall in 1993.

ANOTHER TICKET
(Clapton)

GARY BROOKER'S haunting keyboards introduce this melodic number as Eric opens up with lines that would later transform themselves into 'Behind The Sun' in 1985. Eric's guitar is confined to embellishments only.

I CAN'T STAND IT
(Clapton)

PROBABLY the album's most commercial number. Sadly, when released as a single it failed to sell.

HOLD ME LORD
(Clapton)

GOSPEL style number which features Eric on dobro playing an emotive solo.

FLOATING BRIDGE
(Estes)

WRITTEN in 1940, Eric again shows why he plays the blues like no other white man. Eric took this Sleepy John Estes number and made it his own with appropriate vocals and lilting guitar licks. A short but well executed solo highlights this as one of the better numbers on the album.

CATCH ME IF YOU CAN
(Clapton/Brooker)

CATCHY number about leaving your woman, written in collaboration with Gary Brooker. Eric's double tracked guitars solo over each other in competition.

RITA MAE
(Clapton)

ANOTHER commercial number that features Eric on his beloved Cherry Red Gibson 335 which he's owned since Cream. A fast-paced song that has a repetitive riff as its core base with great drumming from Henry Spinetti. Eric plays a vitriolic solo that is the longest on the album.

Money And Cigarettes

Duck 923773-2; released February 1983
CD: Warners 9362477342, September 2000

ERIC WAS NOT TO RE-APPEAR WITH A NEW ALBUM UNTIL FEBRUARY 1983.
In the intervening two years his lifestyle had changed completely – and
very much for the better. He'd attended Alcoholics Anonymous meetings
in America and kicked alcohol completely, no mean feat for a former
junkie so obviously addicted to one thing or another for the best part of
15 years. Doubtless it had been pointed out to him that he'd probably die
if he continued down the same road. Pattie, however, continued to drink
and their marriage became strained as a result.

Despite Eric's improved health, the sessions were again difficult and
Gary Brooker, Dave Markee and Henry Spinetti were given their march-
ing orders when the first few days of recording proved to be lethargic
and unproductive. A crack team of largely American players was recruited in their place to produce what seemed at first glance to be a delib-
erately commercial album as per the wishes of Eric's record company.

The musicians included the noted slide guitarist and native American music expert Ry Cooder; Duck Dunn, who'd played bass with the
original M.G.s, and Muscle Shoals' stalwart Roger Hawkins who'd
drummed with the last aggregation of Traffic.

With Eric, Albert Lee and Ry Cooder recording together, fans could
be excused for expecting an album that featured plenty of guitar solos,
but this didn't happen. Chris Stainton was kept on, and Tom Dowd again
produced the sessions.

Eric: "I started working on that album with the English rhythm section, but I couldn't get any kick out of them for some reason. The thrill
was gone, and there was a feeling of paranoia in the studio because
they sensed it, too. I spoke to Tom Dowd about it, and he said, 'Just be
brutal. Fire them all, send them all home. They'll understand. And then
we'll bring in some people.' He brought in (bassist Donald) 'Duck' Dunn
and drummer Roger Hawkins, and the first day they came in, we set up
and played 'Crosscut Saw' all day.

"I found I was really getting stretched, and it was the first time I'd
been stretched for several years, simply because I'd been playing with
people who were laying back, and the more I laid back, the more they
laid back. Whereas this rhythm section, they counted themselves off and
started playing, and I didn't have to be there. If I wanted to get in on

it, I had to work fucking hard. And that's when I decided I was getting back to where I should be."

EVERYBODY OUGHTA

MAKE A CHANGE
(Estes)

ANOTHER number by Sleepy John Estes opens Eric's latest album. Backed by a crack studio team Eric plays well, if discreetly. Ry Cooder and Eric are both on slide.

THE SHAPE YOU'RE IN
(Clapton)

TELLING number by Eric which is a great up-tempo song with exciting interplay between him and Albert Lee, who also sings backing vocals.

AIN'T GOING DOWN
(Eric Clapton)

VAGUELY reminiscent of Jimi Hendrix's arrangement of Bob Dylan's 'All Along The Watchtower', Eric soars on guitar and Roger Hawkins holds down the beat admirably.

I'VE GOT A ROCK'N' ROLL HEART
(Seals/Setser/Drummond)

A RATHER lame song that should never have been released as a single. Eric only played it live a handful of times which says it all really.

MAN OVERBOARD
(Clapton)

RY AND Eric again trade on slide for this indifferent song. Pleasant attempt at a commercial sound that Warners were demanding at the time.

PRETTY GIRL
(Clapton)

CERTAINLY the album's most romantic ballad that was surprisingly not released as a single. Eric sings heartfelt lyrics. A rare and beautiful acoustic solo highlights the song.

MAN IN LOVE
(Clapton)

BLUES SHUFFLE that swings nicely. Your foot instinctively taps along to this one as Eric and Ry play slide patterns.

CROSSCUT SAW
(Ford)

ERIC PLAYS his best Albert King licks with some painful string bends. The only criticism is that there is too much Albert and not enough Eric.

SLOW DOWN LINDA
(Clapton)

PLEASANT singalong pub song. Eric and Albert handle the vocals and Eric's solo is short and sweet. In fact, Eric performed the song with Chas and Dave on their 1982 Xmas TV special which was filmed in a makeshift pub.

CRAZY COUNTRY HOP
(Otis)

FAITHFUL cover version of Johnny Otis' 'Crazy Country Hop'. Eric's guitar playing is mainly chord work. Good number to end the album with.

Behind The Sun

Duck 925 166-2; released March 1985
CD: Warners 9362477352, September 2000

PHIL COLLINS, LATELY ENJOYING MASSIVE SUCCESS AS A SOLO PERFORMER at the same time as holding down the drum and vocal spot in Genesis, was drafted in to produce Eric's next album in the hope that he could inject some commercial clout into the grooves. Phil and Eric had known one another for years, and as well as taking a hand in choosing the material Phil also supplied drums on several tracks. Most of the tracks they did together were recorded at Air Studios, Montserrat in the Caribbean.

Warner Brothers clearly wanted a hit album and Eric and Phil did their best to deliver one, but despite their efforts Warners felt that there were no hit singles on the tracks that were handed over. Eric then had the rather humiliating task of recording some new material to order in Los Angeles and the cream of LA's session men were recruited to help, including bassist Nathan East and keyboard player Greg Phillinganes who would eventually play a big role in Eric's career.

Eric: "When the Warner Brothers thing came up, I suddenly realised that the Peter Pan thing was over. Because just before that Van Morrison had been dropped – mightily dropped – and it rang throughout the industry. I thought if they can drop him they can drop me. There was my mortality staring me in the face."

Good as the new material was, the album lacks continuity as a result of shedding some of the original material. And as for Warners finding no singles material on the first version, I suggest that whoever made that decision look for a career change, perhaps working in a cotton bud factory!

The album also sees the return of Jamie Oldaker on drums, while 'Duck' Dunn was retained on bass for some tracks, along with Chris Stainton and Marcy Levy. Albert Lee, never a man to stay in one place for too long, opted out.

Eric: "I wasn't very aware of Genesis; I didn't have any of their records, and wasn't too sure what they were like. It wasn't until I got to know Phil (Collins) that I realised what a good drummer he was and that his tastes in music were akin to mine – the fact that we both like black music the best. I heard the way he was producing John Martyn, and I heard Phil's own things, and I thought I would like to have him produce my record. He's got a great understanding of synthesizers and how they can be used without becoming overpowering.

"We were going more for atmosphere than for a sound, something intangible. Also it was a working relationship that was very creative. I knew it would be easy, from having been around him when he's been making records. We get on very well in the studio; it's a great relationship."

'Behind The Sun' reached a very respectful number eight in the UK and stayed in the charts for 14 weeks.

Eric's worldwide popularity was given a boost by his dignified appearance at Live Aid in Philadelphia the following August. Phil Collins joined his band for the occasion, playing drums alongside Jamie Oldaker.

SHE'S WAITING
(Clapton/Robinson)

THIS POWERFUL opener might have been a hit single had Warners not insisted on 'Forever Man' instead. Phil pounds away at the drums and Eric solos admirably while Marcy Levy makes a welcome return on backing vocals.

SEE WHAT LOVE CAN DO
(Williams)

The first of three songs newly recorded in Los Angeles at the request of Warners. Backed by session men, Eric's sound is drastically altered from the tracks in Montserrat, but this is nevertheless a fine song which is heightened by Eric's exemplary solo.

SAME OLD BLUES
(Clapton)

ONE OF the album's two guitar masterpieces. Eric had not played guitar like this in the studio for many years. Drummer Jamie Oldaker drives Eric on to deliver a red hot solo. Apparently a behind the scenes argument with Phil and the other band members had enraged Eric and this incident added considerable venom to his playing. Eric solos at length up and down the neck on a number that would become the showpiece of his live concerts for many years.

KNOCK ON WOOD
(Floyd/Cropper)

STRAIGHT cover of the great Eddie Floyd Stax soul classic which lacks the zest of the original but became a crowd pleasing encore on the 1985 tour.

SOMETHING'S HAPPENING
(Williams)

THE SECOND of the newly recorded numbers opens with some anthemic powerchord work. Eric's singing is probably more confident than at any other time, and he seems genuinely inspired to play well in the auspicious company of the cream of Los Angeles' session musicians, two of whom would later form part of his band.

FOREVER MAN
(Williams)

THE FIRST single from the album which also involved Eric making his first ever video. A catchy song that only reached number 51 in the charts despite considerable radio play. Short but powerful solo.

IT ALL DEPENDS
(Clapton)

ANOTHER love song written by Eric with a slow lilting solo over a haunting synthesizer backdrop. Good harmonies by Marcy Levy and Shaun Murphy with Ray Cooper on percussion.

TANGLED IN LOVE
(Levy/Feldman)

MARCY'S song suited Eric's style perfectly with its powerful chord changes. Again, synthesizers dominate the song, but Eric does get to play a short, if understated, solo.

NEVER MAKE YOU CRY
(Clapton)

A HAUNTING ballad featuring Eric on a Roland guitar synthesizer. The beautiful solo matches the mood of the song perfectly.

JUST LIKE A PRISONER
(Clapton)

THE ALBUM'S second masterpiece. Those who had complained about the lack of guitar solos on Eric's albums were well and truly placated by this release. Eric's fiery guitar workout is quite spectacular and makes this track one of the best songs he has ever recorded.

BEHIND THE SUN
(Clapton)

RECORDED at Eric's home studio in Ewhurst, Surrey, Eric's tearful vocals give this sad ballad an extra poignancy but it fades out too early. In the live context it was expanded and normally led into 'Wonderful Tonight'.

Eric: "'Behind The Sun' was done at Phil's house, in one take on an eight-track. That's the kind of thing I do when I'm working on little tape machines. I do lots of things like that but never thought of putting them on a record, because I don't think record companies would accept it. I think they only accepted it in this case because it was so short and we snuck it on the end of the album."

August

Duck 925 476-2; released August 1986
CD: Warners 9362477362, September 2000

PHIL COLLINS, BY NOW A HUGELY SUCCESSFUL SOLO STAR IN HIS OWN right, was retained as producer. His commercial touch certainly informed Eric's next album which became his most commercially successful ever. It reached number 3 in the UK charts and stayed in the listings for 47 weeks. Originally titled *One More Car, One More Rider*, it was changed to *August* at the last minute to celebrate the birth of Eric's son, Conor, which coincided with its release.

August was again recorded in Los Angeles and Eric also retained the team of top session players, including Greg Phillinganes and Nathan East, both now permanent fixtures in his entourage. More funky than any of Eric's previous albums, it benefited from Collins' growing awareness of the music that was played on US radio and which sold in bucketloads as a result.

Eric: "People will say that *Behind The Sun* and *August* are Phil Collins records. Fine – if that's all they can hear, they're not listening properly.

I'm in there with as much as I've got, but not in a competitive way. If I did, it would be a mess. It works pretty good for me to allow people to be themselves rather than trying to lay down the law.

"Whenever I make a record my life seems to change yet again. The nature of that depends as much on the influence of the people involved as it does upon the music. It's as if, like a sponge, I absorb the general vibe and the change slowly starts to take place, new patterns of thought, new forms of language, new musical directions, new things to laugh at, and then suddenly it's all over and we have to say good-bye until the next time.

"I think I sold myself a long time ago. I made some kind of deal with myself to get along, to please people, just make life easy, I think. It disturbs me a little to hear myself say that but I have to admit it because otherwise who am I kidding?"

IT'S IN THE WAY THAT YOU USE IT
(Clapton/Robertson)

CO-WRITTEN with Robbie Robertson. The song was recorded at Surrey Sound Studios, Leatherhead, Surrey, as part of the soundtrack for *The Color Of Money* and as such has no place on this record, particularly considering that Warner Brothers removed 'Wanna Make Love To You' to make room for it. Having said that, this song is no slouch and it has some excellent guitar work by Eric who was now playing a new custom built Fender Stratocaster as 'Blackie' had begun to wear out and had taken a well deserved retirement. Featuring a different band and producer, it sounds out of context on the album as a whole.

RUN
(Dozier)

WRITTEN by former Motown specialist Lamont Dozier, 'Run' exemplifies Eric's new sound – tighter, more professional and more commercial. This is only to be expected with a basic band consisting of Phil Collins on drums, Greg Phillinganes on keyboards and Nathan East on bass. All three sing back-up vocals.

TEARING US APART
(Clapton/Phillinganes)

ERIC AND Tina Turner rip it up on a raunchy duet that deserved to be a hit but surprisingly only reached number 53 in the charts. Eric plays a deep slide solo.

BAD INFLUENCE
(Cray/Vannice)

ROBERT Cray and Eric first met at the 1986 Montreux Jazz Festival and they became friends and collaborators over the years. But Eric recorded Robert's 'Bad Influence' before then, and certainly did it justice with his new line-up. A good sax solo by Michael Brecker is followed by a stinging guitar solo that leads the song out. Surprisingly, Eric never played it live.

WALK AWAY
(Levy/Feldman)

ANOTHER Marcy Levy song which would not have sounded out of place on *Behind The Sun*. Eric's echoey vocals plead to a lover not to leave him. Backed by synthesizers, Eric plays delicate guitar fills.

HUNG UP ON YOUR LOVE
(Dozier)

ANOTHER Lamont Dozier song with an uptempo beat unlike anything Eric has recorded before. Again, synthesizers dominate the song, with little guitar to speak of.

TAKE A CHANCE
(Clapton/Phillinganes)

A GREAT funky tune co-written by Eric with Greg. Fabulous horn backing and good vocals by Eric are matched by his solo.

HOLD ON
(Clapton/Collins)

PHIL OPENS this number charging on all cylinders followed by Eric. The sentimental lyrics are sung low in the mix, and Eric's guitar comes into full force only towards the end of the number.

MISS YOU
(Clapton/Phillinganes/Columby)

AN INFECTIOUS up-beat number with a strong R&B feel. Nifty guitar licks and powerful vocals lead into the album's best solo with plenty of the kind of staccato trademark riffs that Eric could knock off in his sleep. The number ends in a volley of guitar breaks that leaves the listener wanting more.

HOLY MOTHER
(Clapton/Bishop)

WRITTEN with his friend Stephen Bishop, this emotive song became a stage favourite and deservedly so. With his own mother clearly in mind, this song features some of Eric's most poignant lyrics matched with a sensitive weeping guitar solo.

BEHIND THE MASK
(Mosdell/Sakamoto/Jackson)

THIS NUMBER had previously been recorded by Greg Phillinganes on his first solo album. Eric liked the arrangement and promptly recorded his version. Released as a single, it was very successful and Eric got to perform it on *Top Of The Pops*. However, this couldn't be further from anything Eric had done before or since.

GRAND ILLUSION
(Robbins/Stephenson/Farrell)

A VAILABLE on the CD version only, this haunting piece features echoey guitar fills over synthesized backing. Eric's solo is inspired and Phil provides his inimitable drum breaks.

Journeyman

CD: Duck 926 074-2; released November 1989

ERIC HAD SO MUCH FUN RECORDING *AUGUST* THAT HE HIRED TWO OF THE session team, Nathan East and Greg Phillinganes, to be part of his band, both for recording and live work. Russ Titleman took over from Phil Collins as producer, and most of the tracks were recorded at The Power Station in New York. Eric had hit a dry spot as far as writing material was concerned, so together with his manager they sifted through potential songs to record for his next album. Jerry Williams again had the lion's share of songs on the album and even turned up to sing some of them with Eric during his Royal Albert Hall shows.

Eric: "I wanted to get Jerry Williams in and the Womacks, because I thought it would be interesting to see how we would marry in the studio. If it would work. It was just an experiment, really, and with the Womacks it worked incredibly well. With Jerry it worked, but we had to confine Jerry, really, to a rhythm part, because he's a wild man. Two years ago I would have been completely submerged by him. My personality up until quite recently would have quite happily stepped aside and let him take the lead role. This time it didn't happen. I was very firm in making sure this record was for me, that I was going to be singing it and that you were going to be accompanying me if you were in the studio. And with someone as strong as Jerry's personality, that's no mean feat.

"We played 'Hound Dog' because Russ (Titleman, the producer) thought it would be a good vehicle for me. And I was like, 'Oh, I don't really know about that, but I'll do it because you think it's a good idea.' And then I thought, 'Well, let's do 'Before You Accuse Me', because I'd always liked the Bo Diddley version. So we tried to do it like that."

PRETENDING
(Williams)

GREG'S SHORT piano intro leads into Eric's strident guitar work. With Phil Collins no longer producing, a new drummer was recruited in Steve Ferrone who is somewhat heavy handed on this number. Jim Keltner would probably have been more suitable. Eric kicks in with some superlative wah-wah solos to please all guitar fans. 'Pretending' was soon to become a live favourite.

ANYTHING FOR YOUR LOVE
(Williams)

ANOTHER classic from Jerry Williams whose writing seemed to suit Eric's vocals perfectly. Eric plays some amazing licks and fills and seems to have fallen in love with the guitar all over again.

BAD LOVE
(Clapton/Jones)

ACCORDING to Eric, Warners wanted another 'Layla', "I thought, well if you sit down and write a song in a formulated way, it's not so hard," he said. Recorded at the Townhouse Studios in London and co-written with Foreigner's Mick Jones, it was a successful single. Its fiery intro led into the first verse, sung with great power by Eric which led into a middle section that came straight from 'Badge'. Eric's string

bend at the start of the solo is simply awesome!

RUNNING ON FAITH
(Williams)

YET ANOTHER great Jerry Williams song. Eric recorded two versions, one with a dobro which is represented here, and another with electric guitar. Both work as well as each other. However, listening to Eric play dobro is always such a great pleasure that this was clearly the right choice.

HARD TIMES
(Charles)

A RAY CHARLES chestnut played by Eric with due reverence. One can imagine being in a small dark intimate club listening to this late at night. Eric struts his stuff over the horn section and his singing is simply staggering.

Eric: "A lot of people have said to me that their favourite track on the album is 'Hard Times'. That really shook me, because I didn't think they would like that. I thought that was almost too ancient in a way, in its approach, for anyone to like it. But there are people out there that want that. And it's very encouraging for me to know that I can make an album in six months' time, or maybe more, that will be comprised of entirely that kind of thing."

HOUND DOG
(Leiber/Stoller)

A STRAIGHT copy of the Elvis Presley hit 'Hound Dog' which sees Eric's manager Roger Forrester making his recording début barking. Eric plays an appropriately dirty slide break.

NO ALIBIS
(Williams)

A STRONG anthemic song that became a live favourite. Eric soars on guitar and listen out for Daryl Hall's harmony vocal.

RUN SO FAR
(Harrison)

G EORGE Harrison contributed several songs but this was the only one that made it on to *Journeyman*. George plays his usual exquisite slide work as Eric sings in best Harrison style.

OLD LOVE
(Clapton/Cray)

P OIGNANT song about an old love who just happened to be Pattie Boyd, his ex-wife. Eric's guitar work continues to mature as the years go by and he hits a definite high on this number. Perhaps it was the presence of Robert Cray that inspired him, but whatever the reason his solo here is excellent. Robert takes the first solo before Eric comes in and takes his turn. Robert takes the number out with Eric's fills.

Eric: "'Old Love'... well, that I wrote with Robert Cray. We'd done these two things, and we had a week of time together. And it was like, 'We've got to do something.' So I started playing the first part of the progression, which is A minor to F to G suspended to G, and then Robert started playing along with me. This was one of those intervals in the studio where no one's doing anything, everyone's kind of lost the thread, and we just started playing this. Robert came up with the turn-around at the end, and then I started writing the words. He wrote 50 percent of the words, and we just did it. It was a perfect collaboration. He took 50 percent of the guitar playing. I took 50 percent. The only thing we didn't share was singing. I wanted to keep that for me. I thought that was one of the best marriages on record that I've done. I think the feeling after we'd done it was, 'Well, we've got it. We've got what we came in here for.'"

BREAKING POINT
(Williams/Grebb)

H EAVY wah-wah intro as Steve Ferrone pounds away on the drums. Eric has clearly taken to the wah-wah again, and this album is choc full of it. David Sanborn plays a great sax solo before Eric wah-wah's away as the song finally fades to his solo guitar.

LEAD ME ON
(Womack/Womack)

ERIC JAMMED with Womack and Womack at Dingwalls club after recording their 'Lead Me On' as a thank you for giving him the song as well as playing on it. Beautifully sung by Eric with Linda Womack, with strings as backing and complemented by a sensitive solo.

BEFORE YOU ACCUSE ME
(McDaniel)

BACK ON more familiar territory, Eric and his band play this R&B number with real feeling together with special guest Robert Cray. Eric plays two exceptional solos.

24 Nights

Duck 7599-26420-2; released December 1991

ERIC WAS CONTRACTED TO RECORD A DOUBLE LIVE ALBUM FOR WARNERS and it seemed logical to record his now regular Royal Albert Hall shows on home turf. Although he performed a record 24 nights in 1991 at the venue, some of the 1990 concerts there were also recorded for inclusion.

This is a very hit and miss affair to say the least. It tries to represent all facets of Eric's shows but fails to represent any adequately. Surely it would have made more sense to release the entire orchestra night as this showed Eric reinventing his hits in a totally new environment. Warners, however, decided against it.

Eric: "Yeah, well, we recorded my shows at the Albert Hall this year and the year before, and we've amalgamated it to make a live record, which is... well, some of it is superb, and some of it isn't superb. It's good, but... I'm very critical of my own performance. I tend to think when I walk offstage that it was brilliant, and then when I listen back to it, I'm not that satisfied. I never am."

BADGE
(Clapton/Harrison)

A VERY Santana-esque intro leads us into more familiar ground when Eric sings the first verse. Features a lively solo. (Recording Date: February 10, 1991).

RUNNING ON FAITH
(Williams)

U NLIKE the studio version which featured a dobro, Eric gives the song the electric treatment with some fiery solos and accompaniment. (RD: January 24, 1990).

WHITE ROOM
(Bruce/Brown)

C REAM'S classic is brought up to date in this exciting version with a stunning wah-wah solo by Eric. (RD: January 24, 1990).

SUNSHINE OF YOUR LOVE
(Bruce/Brown/Clapton)

A NOTHER chance to bring a Cream classic up to date. It must have seemed strange for Eric to be playing this song on the very stage where he played it for the last time with Cream at their final November '68 gig. Listen out for his fancy chord work in the jam section at the end of the song and Steve Ferrone's drum solo. (RD: January 24, 1990).

WATCH YOURSELF
(Guy)

T HE SIGHT of Eric, Buddy Guy and Robert Cray together on stage was a blues lover's dream come true. Sadly, only a few of the songs were released. Robert takes the first solo followed by Buddy as Eric plays rhythm. However, Eric comes in later with a stinging break. (RD: February 5, 1990).

HAVE YOU EVER LOVED A WOMAN?
(Myles)

B LUES at its best. Eric again demonstrates both his vocal and guitar skills. Not quite as passionate as the version found on the *Layla* album, but certainly a highlight of the blues nights. (RD: February 5, 1990).

WORRIED LIFE BLUES
(Merriweather)

O NE OF Eric's favourites, played with due deference to Muddy Waters. Listen to Johnnie Johnson's piano accompaniment and Eric's emotional solo. (RD: February 5, 1990).

HOODOO MAN
(Wells)

T HE ONLY number from the 1991 blues season to be released features Jimmie Vaughan on guitar and Jerry Portnoy on harmonica. Eric's vocals are a highlight as is his hard edged solo. (RD: February 28, 1991).

PRETENDING
(Williams)

PERFECTLY suited to the concert stage, this number enables Eric to unleash some menacing wah-wah solos. (RD: February 18, 1991).

BAD LOVE
(Clapton/Jones)

GREAT SONG but nothing is added to the studio original. (RD: February 18, 1991).

OLD LOVE
(Clapton/Cray)

'OLD LOVE' became the central improvisatory piece in Eric's live set, generally surpassing the original studio version. His searing guitar solo obliterates anything done previously and is certainly one of his best. Greg and Nathan also offer some inspirational solos before Eric calms things down with a lengthy solo before ending the song after some 13 minutes. (RD: February 18, 1991).

WONDERFUL TONIGHT
(Clapton)

A NEW arrangement of this classic piece meant that Eric could keep it sounding fresh by reinventing it every few years. A lengthy, moody keyboard intro led into the more familiar opening chords drawing rapturous applause. The song now featured a sublime call and answer session between Eric on guitar and Katie Kissoon on vocals. (RD: February 18, 1991).

BELL BOTTOM BLUES
(Clapton)

A RARE outing of this cult classic from *Layla*. Played with the National Philharmonic, Eric plays a faithful copy of the original. (RD: February 9, 1990).

HARD TIMES
(Charles)

THE ORCHESTRA backing gives this classic an extra edge, but it does not sound remarkably different from the original. (RD: February 9, 1990).

EDGE OF DARKNESS
(Clapton/Kamen)

ONE OF Eric's most haunting pieces – this one written for an absorbing TV mini-series about impropriety in the nuclear industry – is given a chilling backing by the orchestra. Eric plays sublime lines over the violins and builds into a rising crescendo of notes before playing a frenzied solo. (RD: March 8th, 1991).

Unplugged

Duck 9362-45024-2; released August 1992

MTV'S *UNPLUGGED* SESSIONS, WHERE ARTISTS WOULD PLAY PURELY acoustic sets, proved to be among the most popular TV rock programmes ever. A host of top stars from several generations of rock, including Paul McCartney, Rod Stewart, Nirvana and more, duly unplugged themselves, though some, notably Bruce Springsteen, insisted on bringing their amps. Eric was an obvious candidate and he played a marvellous two hour set at Bray Studios near Windsor, on January 16, 1992.

Although Eric enjoyed the experience, he felt it would not be wise to release it on record, assuming it would appeal only to a niche market. He was never wider of the mark, and was more surprised than anybody when it subsequently became his biggest selling album ever, resulting in a handful of Grammy Awards.

Eric: "There's not much I can say about these songs, except that they helped me through a very, very hard patch in my life."

Eric's band for the *Unplugged* session included his old friend Andy Fairweather-Low on extra guitar, bassist Nathan East, Steve Ferrone on drums, with Ray Cooper banging away on extra percussion, and Chuck Leavell on piano.

SIGNE
(Clapton)

ONE OF several songs Eric wrote while mourning the death of his son. Named after the boat on which it was written, this is a samba style instrumental played on a gut string guitar.

BEFORE YOU ACCUSE ME
(McDaniel)

GIVEN AN acoustic blues treatment with a short solo.

HEY HEY
(Broonzy)

ONE OF the songs Eric used to sing on the folk club and pub circuit in the early Sixties. Andy Fairweather-Low accompanies Eric on guitar.

TEARS IN HEAVEN
(Clapton/Jennings)

ERIC'S HEARTFELT song about his son Conor, who had died tragically on March 20, 1991. On the video Eric is visibly moved at the end of the first public hearing of this intensely personal song. Again played on gut string acoustic.

Eric: "On occasions it's been close to where I would choke and not be able to do it... but then what would happen? We'd have to stop and it would get mawkish and embarrassing. At the same time to back off and pretend that it's about nothing and just play it as if it's a song that had no meaning would be pointless, so there's a thin line you have to tread, somewhere in the middle."

LONELY STRANGER
(Clapton)

ANOTHER song written about Conor and previewed here. Slow lilting number with sympathetic backing from the band.

NOBODY KNOWS YOU WHEN YOU'RE DOWN AND OUT
(Cox)

PERFECT setting for this version that was previously found on the *Layla* album in a roaring electric version. Here, Eric gives it an almost barrelhouse feel. Eric taps his foot and plays a good guitar solo on a steel string guitar. Great backing vocals from Katie Kissoon and Tessa Niles.

LAYLA
(Clapton/Gordon)

PETE TOWNSHEND jokingly called this Eric's karaoke version. However, it is interesting to hear this classic piece played in almost waltz time.

RUNNING ON FAITH
(Williams)

GOOD version which sounds like its original as it again features Eric on dobro.

WALKIN' BLUES
(Robert Johnson)

ERIC GETS to play Robert Johnson. His vocals are very authentic and he plays a mean bottleneck solo.

ALBERTA
(Trad. arr. Ledbetter)

A WELCOME return of this number which Eric had played during the 1976 and 1977 tours. The band again join him for this number.

SAN FRANCISCO BAY BLUES
(Fuller)

ANOTHER of the songs Eric used to perform on the folk club and pub circuit in the early Sixties. It's audience participation time as Eric and his band clearly have fun with the kazoos.

MALTED MILK
(Johnson)

STUNNING vocals on the second Robert Johnson number of the set. Played on a steel-stringed acoustic.

OLD LOVE
(Clapton/Cray)

WONDERFUL live version in this acoustic setting. Eric plays and sings with great passion and his solo is quite awe inspiring.

ROLLIN' AND TUMBLIN'
(Waters)

SADLY, this number was totally impromptu during a short break in the filming. Eric suddenly started jamming which quickly developed into 'Rollin' And Tumblin". Unfortunately, neither the cameras nor the tape machines were operating. Obviously, when the technicians realised this was developing into a full blown number they quickly turned everything on, which is why only half appears on the disc. It was totally unrehearsed.

From The Cradle

Duck 9362-45735-2; released September 1994

AS THE FOREMOST WHITE BLUES GUITARIST OF HIS GENERATION, ERIC HAD considered recording an all-blues album on several occasions, but it took the success of *Unplugged* to convince him that there was an audience out there eager to hear it.

The other musicians at the sessions at Olympic included: drummer Jim Keltner, Jerry Portnoy on harp, bassist Dave Bronze (who plays in a Southend band called The Hamsters), Andy Fairweather-Low on guitar and Chris Stainton on keyboards. Eric co-produced it with Warners Brothers staff production chief Russ Titelman.

Eric: "I was actually trying as hard as I could to try and replicate [the original recordings]. But it still came out as me which is the beauty of the whole exercise. I used to think that pure imitation was not good enough but of course there is no such thing.

"It's taken me a lot of courage to go back. I mean... I'm retracing my steps back to John Mayall and the Bluesbreakers. I'd come to John Mayall from a pop band that had started as a blues band, The Yardbirds. And then when I was leaving Mayall, in my head I was going to an even more hardcore blues situation which backfired. And now what I'm doing is going back to that jumping-off point. It's almost like I'm just leaving John Mayall now and I'm producing my own blues band. And it's taken me 30 years of meandering the back streets to get there."

BLUES BEFORE SUNRISE
(Carr)

IS IT ERIC or Elmore? Rollicking slide intro and gruff vocals are the order of the day as Eric displays his best studio playing since the days of the Bluesbreakers. Eric's slide solo is well constructed and clearly played live, as indeed was most of the album.

THIRD DEGREE
(Boyd/Dixon)

ERIC PLAYS some warm chords and short solo bursts and licks. Again, his vocals are exemplary and Chris Stainton's piano playing is quite a revelation.

RECONSIDER BABY
(Fulson)

AUTHENTIC cover with a wild guitar intro. Eric sings so well on this album that it is difficult to pick a track where he sings better than on all the others. His solo here is in the fine tradition of the blues.

HOOCHIE COOCHIE MAN
(Dixon)

ERIC PLAYS this as Muddy did, mean and moody. Jerry Portnoy shines on harmonica.

FIVE LONG YEARS
(Boyd)

A SEARING lead break opens this blues classic, as Eric pleads his case on vocals. A valve-rattling solo spits out off the speakers and pins the listeners against their seat. One of the many highlights.

I'M TORE DOWN
(Thompson)

ERIC GETS to be Freddie King, one of his early influences on electric guitar. Every bit as good as anything on the *Bluesbreakers* album.

HOW LONG BLUES
(Carr)

ERIC GETS unplugged and changes over to dobro and acoustic guitar for Leroy Carr's 'How Long'. Nice harmonica solo by Jerry Portnoy.

GOIN' AWAY BABY
(Lane)

BLUES shuffle that features a solo that evokes the original piece.

BLUES LEAVE ME ALONE
(Lane)

ERIC PLAYS a typical blues anthem and ends up sounding like Muddy Waters and his band. Jerry Portnoy blows a storm.

SINNER'S PRAYER
(Glenn/Fulson)

ERIC'S BAND demonstrate what a tight unit they are with some fine playing. Jim Keltner, together with the horn section, shine in particular. Eric plays some sparing guitar breaks.

MOTHERLESS CHILD
(Traditional)

UNPLUGGED again, with 12-string acoustic guitar and mandolin, Eric is clearly enjoying himself on this number that became the first single off the album.

IT HURTS ME TOO
(James)

APOCALYPTIC slide break opens this thunderous version of Elmore James' 'It Hurts Me Too'. Grungy chord work leads into some superlative slide work and Eric sings with his now customary gruffness.

SOMEDAY AFTER A WHILE
(King/Thompson)

ANOTHER Freddie King number on which Eric shines. Using a beautiful Gibson Les Paul, Eric plays a solo plucked from heaven. Notes just keep on falling out of nowhere. Stunning!

STANDIN' ROUND CRYING
(Waters)

FAITHFUL cover of one of Eric's favourite Muddy Waters songs. Both Eric and Jerry Portnoy even shout out Muddy's original asides. That's OK, though, as Jerry played in Muddy's band and Eric was his 'adopted son'.

DRIFTIN'
(Brown/Moore/Williams)

UNPLUGGED again for this fine interpretation of a song that Eric had played live on his 1974 US tour and which appeared on the resultant *EC Was Here* album.

GROANING THE BLUES
(Dixon)

THE ALBUM'S *pièce de résistance*. Eric simply has not played better at any time in his long and illustrious career. Here is a man clearly enjoying himself and playing what he chooses.

Pilgrim

Reprise 9362465772, released March 1998

ERIC HAD MADE VARIOUS ATTEMPTS AT RECORDING THIS ALBUM, BUT felt unhappy with the results. He took on producer Simon Climie to take on the production duties with him, and the sessions developed from there. *Pilgrim* was recorded in London and Los Angeles, and it contains several covers with contemporary arrangements. There is a rendition of the blues lament 'Going Down Slow' by St. Louis Jimmy and 'Born In Time' by Bob Dylan. In fact, the production was very much of its time and was probably done so with a view of introducing a whole new generation of fans to Eric's music.

The album is also remarkable for the noticeable change in Eric's vocals. This is partially because he had given up smoking and partially due to the influence of Babyface on the hit single, 'Change The World.' Eric's vocals have a major Curtis Mayfield vibe about them, which alienated a lot of his fan base, while introducing him to new fans who liked classy contemporary pop music.

Clapton does not like to get stuck in a rut. He is constantly looking forward with the occasional look back. So with this album, gone is the intimacy of *Unplugged*, as Eric worked with synth keyboards, drum samples and pro-tools courtesy of Simon Climie. He recalls that "we really loved making *Pilgrim*, where we just holed up in the studio and did most of it without any help from any musicians. It was all machines and, just making fabrics and ideas out of nothing." A 20-piece orchestra also featured on several of the 14 cuts, and Eric even took a small orchestra on the road with him to replicate the sound.

However much the production might annoy some folk, the fact remains that this album features some of Eric's best songs in years. Some of the gems on display here include the lead-off single, 'My Father's Eyes' along with 'Circus,' a poignant ballad written about his late son that had featured on the original television broadcast of *Unplugged*.

Pilgrim is also a long album clocking in at over 72 minutes.

MY FATHER'S EYES
(Clapton)

SLICK OPENER featuring some nice dobro playing set against a backdrop of machines. Strong vocal from Eric.

RIVER OF TEARS
(Clapton/Climie)

SLOW HAUNTING track that would not be out of place on a suitable film soundtrack. Once again, Eric's vocals are incredibly emotive. When he sings about drowning in a river of tears, you believe him. Subtle orchestration suits the mood perfectly. Listen out for the slide solo.

PILGRIM
(Clapton/Climie)

A REASONABLE love song, marred by the monotonous backing track, but redeemed slightly by Eric's soulful vocals.

BROKEN HEARTED
(Clapton/Phillinganes)

PREVIEWED on the Japanese tour in 1997, 'Broken Hearted' is co-written by ex-bandmate Greg Phillinganes. He had previously written 'Behind the Mask', which was a surprise hit for Eric back in the late Eighties. Broken Hearted is yet another insipid ballad, saved by a good vocal performance.

ONE CHANCE
(Clapton/Climie)

NICE FUNKY bass line punctuated by some stunning guitar work and a powerful vocal makes this a standout track.

CIRCUS
(Clapton)

BEAUTIFUL song about Eric's late son that was played in concert as early as 1992. One of several songs Eric wrote in Antigua after the death of Conor, it tells the story of what father and son had been doing the week before the tragic accident. The arrangement of the original song still stands and is better for it.

GOING DOWN SLOW
(Jimmy)

BLUES CLASSIC, but done with a completely different arrangement to the original. This version has a hip-hop backing drum track with Eric soloing over the top of it. Once again, inspired vocals.

FALL LIKE RAIN
(Clapton)

A MODERN day version of 'Lay Down Sally' is the best way to describe this tune. Surprisingly, it does not feel out of place despite its country groove. Nice guitar picking.

BORN IN TIME
(Dylan)

DOBRO-laden cover of a modern Dylan classic from his *Under The Red Sky* album. Sounds like the perfect Eric Clapton song.

SICK AND TIRED
(Clapton/Climie)

ERIC WACKS out the electric for this quirky blues tune. Inane lyrics about buying a parrot and getting it to learn how to remember a girl's name etc. Go figure. Nice guitar work though and a bit of light relief from the clinical production work of most of the other tracks.

NEEDS HIS WOMAN
(Clapton)

GENTLE acoustic love song very much in the mould of his Babyface-produced 'Change The World' single.

SHES'S GONE
(Clapton/Climie)

THE ALBUM highlight and a firm live favourite on the *Pilgrim* tour that followed the album's release.

YOU WERE THERE
(Clapton/Climie)

THIS EMOTIVE song was written by Eric for his ex-manager Roger Forrester. They parted ways after nearly 25 years in 1998, apparently because of Eric's increased interest in his own Crossroads rehabilitation centre. The lyrics say it all really. Eric and Roger in particular, went through a lot together and by some miracle survived with their sanity pretty much intact. The song is a celebration of that fact and a thank you to his manager for sticking by him through it all. Wonderful song and inspired guitar work.

INSIDE OF ME
(Clapton/Climie)

BACK TO the hip-hop influenced drum loops and samples again. Strings make their presence felt and Eric is again in Curtis mode. The song offers up a nice groove and a good funky solo. Eric's daughter, Ruth contributes some spoken words towards the tail end of the number.

Eric in the garden of his Ripley home, around 1970.
(Graham Wiltshire/Redferns)

Eric on stage at Crystal Palace, July 31, 1976. *(Andre Csillag/Rex Features)*

On tour in the US, 1978.
(Neal Preston/Corbis)

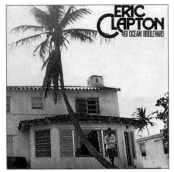

461 Ocean Boulevard (1974)

With Jeff Beck at the September 1983 Arms Concert at London's Royal Albert Hall. *(Roger Ressmeyer/Corbis)*

Money And Cigarettes (1983)

Eric on stage with Lionel Ritchie in 1987. *(LFI)*

Mark Knopfler of Dire Straits duets with Eric during Free Nelson Mandala concert at Wembley Stadium, June 11, 1988. *(Lynn Goldsmith/Corbis)*

Journeyman (1989)

24 Nights (1991)

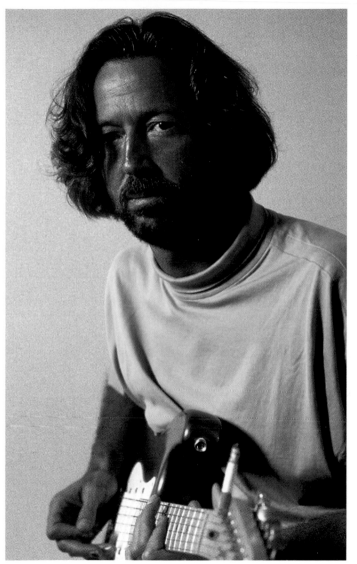

Eric in 1990. *(LFI)*

Unplugged (1992)

Eric collects five Grammy Awards, February 24, 1993. *(Reuters/Corbis)*

On stage at the Royal Albert Hall, February 18, 1996. *(LFI)*

At the Birmingham NEC in 1998. *(LFI)*

Eric shares the mike with Bob Dylan at Madison Square Garden, June 30, 1999, at a benmefot show for Clapton's 'Crossroads' rehabilitation centre in Antigua. *(LFI)*

Cream BBC Sessions (2003)

On stage at the Tsunami Relief Concert at the Millennium Stadium, Cardiff, January 22, 2005. *(LFI)*

"How long have you been playing the guitar," asked the Queen, as she gave Eric his MBE. "About 40 years ma'am," he replied.
(James Patrick Cooper/Retna)

Riding With The King

Reprise 9362476122, released June 2000

Eric Clapton and B.B. King had been pussyfooting around the fact that they should record an album together for years. They first jammed together in New York at the Cafe Au Go Go in 1967. Over the next 30 plus years they had often played together, but a joint album remained elusive. Until now, that is.

Getting two independently well-known artists together on one album is always a good way of generating audience interest. And on this album, we have a very high profile blues collaboration, which was initiated by the artists themselves, resulting in some sparkling music.

It was Clapton who found a window in his schedule and approached B.B. about finally doing the deed. B.B was all in favour and came off the road for a month in January and February 2000 for the joint recording. Clapton evidently chose the songs, subject to approval by King. Some of these include some of B.B's best-known tunes along with some pieces by Texas guitarist Doyle Bramhall II. The high points are definitely the guitar exchanges between these two veterans, who spend no time at all in shedding any sense of professional discretion with some stinging exchanges.

RIDING WITH THE KING
(Hiatt)

THE TITLE song written by John Hiatt for his 1983 *Riding WIth The King* album. Apt title, but the song is probably more familiar to Clapton than B.B. due to its rocky sound. None the less, the CD gets off to an energetic start.

TEN LONG YEARS
(King/Bihari)

THE CD now moves straight into blues mode with 'Ten Long Years', a faithful remake of a

King composition that B.B. has been playing for years. It gives both guitarists a chance for some great playing.

KEY TO THE HIGHWAY
(Broonzy/Seger)

A DEFINITE highlight. This version is the first of two acoustic tracks on the album. Big Bill Broonzy's blues standard from the Thirties is no stranger to Clapton who previously recorded it as part of the Derek & The Dominos' *Layla* album nearly 30 years ago. He also played it live for many years after. B.B admitted he was not fond of acoustics, but said: "Eric suggested that we do an unplugged thing. I wasn't too happy about it at first (*laughs*). But when we sat down and started to do it, I was tickled to death. I enjoyed it very much. So that was a change. And once we got into it, it was really fun because I hadn't done that in years. In fact, only once in my career have I done an unplugged tune. It was many years ago with Alexis Korner. We did something called 'Alexis Boogie' on the album *Live In London*. And that's the only time I ever did acoustic guitar on the record."

MARRY YOU
(Bramhall II/Melvoin/Ross)

GREAT funky rock tune that sounds like the whole studio is having fun. Again, this sounds more like Eric's territory, rather than BB's. A very catchy number, with a great solo, this should have been the single.

THREE O'CLOCK BLUES
(King/Bihari)

A REMAKE of B.B. King's first national R&B hit. Eric starts out singing this slow blues, before B.B joins in with some exceptional vocals. The two guitar solos are absolute killers.

HELP THE POOR
(Singleton)

ORIGINALLY from the B.B. King repertoire, this can be found on the classic 1965 *Live At The Regal* album. This number has a wonderfully funky New Orleans groove to it. Nice Jimmy Vaughan solo.

I WANNA BE
(Bramhall II/Sexton)

WRITTEN by the guitar aces in Arc Angles. A suitably funky number that sounds tailormade for the two guitar gods. Vocals are shared between Eric and BB. Great guitar work by Doyle Bramhall II.

WORRIED LIFE BLUES
(Merriweather)

THE SECOND acoustic track is an old favourite of Eric's. Interesting to hear both of these blues giants playing acoustically.

DAYS OF OLD
(King/Bihari)

GREAT boogie shuffle. B.B. King clearly loves this one and the whole band are cooking.

WHEN MY HEART BEATS LIKE A HAMMER
(King/Bihari)

SLOW BLUES, and another highlight. The boys get low down

and dirty on this one and give it all they have.

HOLD ON I'M COMIN'
(Hayes/Porter)

A STAX favourite that was originally a hit for Sam and Dave. This is perhaps an odd choice for a blues album with its obvious Memphis soul groove, but it works.

COME RAIN OR COME SHINE
(Mercer/Arlen)

BEAUTIFUL old standard recorded by Ray Charles. B.B. King had some reservations about doing this, but it ends up being a nice sedate way to end the album.

Reptile

Reprise 9362479662, released March 2001

ERIC'S *REPTILE* ALBUM IS DEDICATED TO HIS UNCLE ADRIAN AND AUNT, Sylvia Clapp. These relatives along with memories of his childhood in Ripley, Surrey, are the main inspiration on the record.

In his liner notes, Eric writes that his Uncle Adrian died in the spring of 2000, just as Eric was beginning work on the album: "He was a fine man, very gifted and wildly creative, an important member of our family, and the community." He goes on to say, "In those early days I was given to believe that he was my brother, and as a result he had an incredibly profound effect on my view of the world... I realise now that most of my tastes in music, art, clothes, cars, etc., etc., were formed in this period of my life and were due mostly to the wonderful relationship I had with my uncle Adrian."

It is well documented that Eric was raised by his grandparents, whom he believed were his parents until he was told the devastating truth as a teenager. He also notes that the term "reptile" is not an insult, but rather "a term of endearment" in his childhood home. He confirms that his Uncle Adrian was "the greatest reptile of them all". High praise indeed. The album-closing instrumental "Son & Sylvia" is his touching tribute to his aunt and uncle.

Clapton recorded *Reptile* with a band that included Billy Preston, Paul Carrack, and Doyle Bramhall II, along with backing vocals from The Impressions, who, of course, featured the late Curtis Mayfield for many years.

Reptile has its fair share of cover songs, including James Taylor's 'Don't Let Me Be Lonely Tonight', Stevie Wonder's 'I Ain't Gonna Stand For It', J.J. Cale's 'Travelin' Light' and Ray Charles' 'Come Back Baby'.

REPTILE
(Clapton)

SOFT BRAZILIAN flavoured acoustic instrumental and a mood-setting opener.

GOT YOU ON MY MIND
(Thomas/Biggs)

ENJOYABLE shuffle that would become a live favourite on the accompanying tour.

TRAVELIN' LIGHT
(Cale)

FAITHFUL JJ Cale cover. Eric plays a great slide solo.

BELIEVE IN LIFE
(Clapton)

NICE GUITAR intro leading into a number not too distant from 'Change The World.'

Nice gospel feel to it also, thanks to the presence of The Impressions.

COME BACK BABY
(Charles)

ERIC IS IN stunning vocal form on this one – his singing just keeps on getting better and better as he gets older. Killer guitar

solo and one that should have been played live.

BROKEN DREAMS
(Climie/Morgan)

SLICK acoustic guitar-driven number that sounds remarkably like the soulful tones of Robert Cray.

FIND MYSELF
(Clapton)

A GREAT late night blues/jazz feel prevails throughout this good time number.

I AIN'T GONNA STAND FOR IT
(Wonder)

ERIC HAS been a fan of Stevie Wonder since his early years. He even did a session for Stevie in 1971. This catchy cover was clearly fun for Eric to do and was also issued as a single and became a live favourite for a time.

I WANT A LITTLE GIRL
(Mencher/Moll)

ANOTHER highlight. Gentle piano intro leads into some soft melodic guitar work from EC. Once again, his vocals are stellar.

Eric still performs this during his tours.

SECOND NATURE
(Clapton/Climie/Morgen)

A FUNKY Tony Joe White swamp groove goes throughout this number. Eric plays some subtle slide work and The Impressions provide their incomparable backing voices.

DON'T LET ME BE LONELY TONIGHT
(Taylor)

S ENSITIVE James Taylor ballad sung beautifully by Eric. A gospel feel prevails thanks to The Impressions and Eric throws in some impressive licks as well as a solo of note.

MODERN GIRL
(Clapton)

O RIGINALLY recorded for the *Pilgrim* album and left off but now re-recorded. Gentle acoustic based number about not throwing ones' love away.

SUPERMAN INSIDE
(Clapton/Bramhall II)

A GREAT collaboration between these two guitarists. It has Eric's pop sensibilities blending with Doyle's more rootsy approach, giving the listener a genuinely exciting song.

SON & SYLVIA
(Clapton)

N ICE ACOUSTIC instrumental that is the album's gentle closer. Reminiscent of 'Behind The Sun', it features a Stevie Wonder-like harmonica solo by Billy Preston.

One More Car, One More Rider

Reprise 9362483972, released November 2002

O NE MORE CAR, ONE MORE RIDER IS A DOUBLE LIVE ALBUM RECORDED during Eric's 2001 *Reptile* tour at the Budokan in Tokyo and the Staples Center in Los Angeles. *One More Car, One More Rider* was originally the name for Eric's 1986 album *August*. It was changed at the last minute to celebrate the month of the birth of his son Conor.

KEY TO THE HIGHWAY
(Broonzy/Seger)

ERIC STEPS onto the stage alone, sits down on a chair, is handed his Martin acoustic and performs a superb version of 'Key To The Highway'.

REPTILE
(Clapton)

ERIC IS joined by the rest of his band to play the title track of his latest studio album. More lively than the studio version, Eric plays a blinding jazz-tinged solo.

GOT YOU ON MY MIND
(Thomas/Biggs)

A LIVE FAVOURITE on the tour, it has the added bonus of an interesting solo by Andy Fairweather-Low. Eric is again in fine vocal form.

TEARS IN HEAVEN
(Clapton)

SAME arrangement as found on *Unplugged*.

BELL BOTTOM BLUES
(Clapton)

ALWAYS A welcome addition to any show, Eric has played this fan favourite from the *Layla* album every now and again and on this tour he plays it acoustically.

CHANGE THE WORLD
(Kennedy/Kirkpatrick/Sims)

A HIT SINGLE that became a regular in the set for this tour. It sticks close to the studio version, but does have an inspired acoustic solo.

FATHER'S EYES
(Clapton)

POIGNANT number from the *Pilgrim* album, Eric is back on electric for this one and plays a beautifully melodic intro to the song.

RIVER OF TEARS
(Clapton/Climie)

A NOTHER *Pilgrim* number which sounds much more powerful and grander live than in the studio. Eric is on fine form on the solo.

GOING DOWN SLOW
(Jimmy)

UP-TEMPO version of blues classic that follows the studio version pretty closely. Nice guitar solo though.

SHE'S GONE
(Clapton/Climie)

HIGH POWERED live favourite with some unbelievable guitar solos. Far superior to the studio version.

I WANT A LITTLE GIRL
(Mencher/Moll)

SMOKEY blues at its best with fantastic keyboard work.

BADGE
(Clapton/Harrison)

THE OLD Cream favourite.

HOOCHIE COOCHIE MAN
(Dixon)

A LEFT OVER from the 'From The Cradle' tour and clearly a fun experience for both the band and audience alike. Some sterling guitar work from Eric here.

HAVE YOU EVER LOVED A WOMAN?
(Myles)

A NOTHER blues gem that can originally be found on the *Layla* album. This is probably the best guitar extravaganza track on this live album.

COCAINE
(Cale)

GUARANTEED to get the crowd on their feet.

WONDERFUL TONIGHT
(Clapton)

OUT COME the lighters!

LAYLA
(Clapton/Gordon)

THE CLAPTON classic. One of the most powerful love songs ever written and still performed with passion.

SUNSHINE OF YOUR LOVE
(Clapton/Bruce/Brown)

A NOTHER Cream classic. Eric would play this number fairly regularly over the years after ignoring it for a long while.

OVER THE RAINBOW
(Arlen/Harburg)

ERIC GOES into sentimental mode with mixed results. But, it was a nice gentle way to send the public home at the end of the show.

Me And Mr Johnson

Reprise 936248730, released March 2004

ROBERT **J**OHNSON **WAS THE LEGENDARY** **T**HIRTIES **BLUESMAN WHO** according to legend made a deal with the devil at the crossroads which enabled him to play the guitar better than anyone else. He wrote a mere 29 songs and 14 of those appear on this tribute to the man who influenced the music of Eric Clapton more than any other individual over the years. Eric remembers his first reaction on hearing Johnson: "It was so powerful it was almost unlistenable at first."

Eric's album of Robert Johnson covers is a fascinating juxtaposition of old blues songs done with electric instruments, using modern production values. Interestingly, this album almost never came about. Eric had in fact been in the studio laying down ideas for his next pop release. However, things were not going well and during 'down' time, both he and the band would jam on some Robert Johnson stuff. Eric told his producer to let the tapes roll and before long, the fun jams turned into a new project. Eric recalls the conversation, "I've got this idea, while we're trying to do this album, whenever we get a break, let's do a Robert Johnson song. Just for fun, just to see, 'cause maybe, you know, it'll take the strain off of what we're really trying to do."

It's amazing to think that this collection of Robert Johnson covers is only Eric Clapton's second all-blues album as a solo artist in more than 30 years. He often dipped his toe in Johnson territory, such as his now legendary performance of 'Crossroads' with Cream. Then, over the years, versions of 'Ramblin' On My Mind', 'I'm A Steady Rollin' Man', 'Malted Milk', 'Walkin' Blues' and 'Kind Hearted Woman Blues'. I suspect that this album will be remembered more for Eric's vocals than anything else.

WHEN YOU GOT A GOOD
(Johnson)

A DECENT shuffling rocker in the vein of 'Before You Accuse Me' found on Eric's *Journeyman* album.

LITTLE QUEEN OF SPADES
(Johnson)

SOLID orchestration and an expressive guitar solo with Eric in fine form on vocals also.

THEY'RE RED HOT
(Johnson)

ERIC AND the band get a great New Orleans rag time vibe on this one. Billy Preston shows off his amazing keyboard skills and Jerry Portnoy blows a mean harp solo. This was a favourite on the tour that promoted the album.

ME AND THE DEVIL BLUES
(Johnson)

GREAT, moody acoustic arrangement.

TRAVELLING RIVERSIDE BLUES
(Johnson)

THE RHYTHM section provides an authentic, bottomless thump to this stomping blues tune. Doyle Bramhall II supplies some tasty slide licks.

LAST FAIR DEAL GONE DOWN
(Johnson)

SHORT, snappy, jaunty sing-a-long with solid backing from all the band.

STOP BREAKIN' DOWN BLUES
(Johnson)

SOLID electric version with sterling vocals from Eric.

MILK COW BLUES
(Johnson)

SLIDE driven version that shuffles along nicely.

KIND HEARTED WOMAN BLUES
(Johnson)

PERFORMED live in Glasgow in 1978 as a one-off, now at long last we get a dark, slow version in the studio. Eric is in fine form on vocals. Doyle Bramhall II provides some tasty licks and is the perfect foil for Eric who punctuates the number with a nice solo.

COME ON IN MY KITCHEN
(Johnson)

ERIC HAD performed this a few times in concert during 1994 as a solo acoustic piece. He sticks pretty close to that original arrangement and it's certainly one of the album's highlights.

IF I HAD POSSESSION OVER JUDGEMENT DAY
(Johnson)

AT FIRST you could be forgiven thinking that this was 'Rollin' And Tumblin'. But no, it's a similar arrangement with a stomping blues vibe to it.

LOVE IN VAIN
(Johnson)

PROBABLY the most famous cover version of this song is by The Rolling Stones on their classic 1969 *Let It Bleed* album. Eric sticks mainly to the original Johnson arrangement.

32-20 BLUES
(Johnson)

GREAT piano work from Billy Preston and the band are really tight on this rockabilly arrangement.

HELLHOUND ON MY TRAIL
(Johnson)

GOOD version, but it nevertheless fails to conjure up the spare, haunting dread of the original, where you really believe Johnson has the hounds of hell at his door.

PART SIX
COMPILATIONS
Crossroads

Polydor 8352612, released April 1988

AFTER ERIC'S PUBLIC RESURGENCE IN **1985** AS A RESULT OF LIVE AID AND several other high profile charity events, it seemed logical to compile a multi-track career retrospective. *Crossroads* was clearly aimed at those fans who had perhaps lost interest in Eric over the years, and to give new fans an opportunity to catch up with his past. *The Cream Of Eric Clapton* was released in September 1987 and included all of his better known numbers from Cream, Derek & The Dominos and the solo years, including several tracks licensed from Warner Brothers. This album remained high on the charts for several months and was a constant seller until Polygram released the 4CD *Crossroads* set in April 1988.

Lovingly compiled by producer Bill Levenson, *Crossroads* went on to become one of the best selling retrospective box sets ever and Levenson was awarded a Grammy for his efforts. The four CDs spanned Eric's entire career from The Yardbirds' early demos to a re-recording of 'After Midnight' in 1987, and included a slew of unreleased material for the benefit of serious Clapton collectors.

The tracks not already dealt with above are as follows:

THE YARDBIRDS

BOOM BOOM
(Hooker)

HONEY IN YOUR HIPS
(Relf)

BABY WHAT'S WRONG
(Reed)

THREE early Yardbirds demos, recorded at R.G. Jones' Studio at Morden in Surrey during February 1964 which were hawked around record companies to secure the band a deal. Despite their raw sound, they display a youthful optimism and they perform their sole original song with the same enthusiasm as they reproduce the covers of John Lee Hooker and Jimmy Reed. But there is nothing here to suggest that their guitarist would become a guitar hero within a year or two.

CREAM

LAWDY MAMA
(Trad. arr. Clapton)

RECORDED for BBC Radio in December 1966, this is the original version of 'Lawdy Mama' as opposed to the one that was basically a revamp of 'Strange Brew', released on the *Live Cream* album. Raw blues at its best.

STEPPIN' OUT
(Bracken)

ANOTHER BBC recording, this one taped in January 1967. An excellent version, with Eric on top form on the solo. Both tracks were later released on the *Cream BBC Sessions* CD in 2003.

BLIND FAITH

SLEEPING IN THE GROUND
(Myers)

RECORDED at Morgan Studios, London during June 1969, this song was originally intended for the *Blind Faith* album but was left off for space reasons. A Sam Myers blues romp which Blind Faith played live at most of their concerts.

ERIC CLAPTON

AFTER MIDNIGHT
(Cale)

A SLIGHTLY different mix from the version of 'After Midnight' recorded on Eric's first solo album with Delaney & Bonnie and Friends.

DEREK AND THE DOMINOS

TELL THE TRUTH
(Clapton/Whitlock)

ROLL IT OVER
(Clapton/Whitlock)

THE ORIGINAL Phil Spector production of the Dominos' first single was withdrawn after a few days in 1970 because Eric was dissatisfied with the sound. Spector's production, done at Abbey Road Studios in August 1970 during the sessions for George Harrison's *All Things Must Pass* album, is awash in his trademark echo, and was obviously incompatible with the sound that the Dominos were trying to achieve.

GOT TO GET BETTER IN A LITTLE WHILE
(Clapton)

FOR THE Clapton aficionado, the most fascinating tracks on the entire *Crossroads* set are those which were recorded at Olympic Studios, Barnes during April 1971 for the aborted second Dominos' album. This song was a stage favourite during the band's only US tour and was generally played as the opening number. Strangely, the studio version was recorded after it had been tried out in concert. There's some nice wah-wah guitar from Eric but the band sound sluggish and uninspired. The live version, found on the live Dominos' album, is far superior.

EVIL
(Dixon)

ANOTHER track from the aborted second album, this is a faithful cover with the band on good form, particularly drummer Jim Gordon. Eric offers a convincing vocal performance and some inspired slide work.

ONE MORE DANCE
(Clapton)

A LOVELY example of Eric on acoustic slide guitar and vocals which definitely deserved to be released earlier. Also from the aborted second album.

MEAN OLD FRISCO
(Crudup)

SIMILAR in style to 'One More Dance', Eric and his Dominos tackle the song acoustically until Eric steps forth for a wah-wah solo. This was later re-recorded by Eric for his *Slowhand* album in 1977.

SNAKE LAKE BLUES
(Clapton/Whitlock)

THE FINAL track from the aborted second Dominos' album is probably the best of the lot, a lilting instrumental electric blues workout that features Eric at every fret on the neck of his Stratocaster.

AIN'T THAT LOVIN' YOU
(Reed)

ONE OF many, mainly blues, outtakes from the *461 Ocean Boulevard* sessions at Criteria Studios, Miami in April 1974. So many extra tracks of quality were recorded that Eric could clearly have released a double album. His anxiety to shed his 'guitar hero' image is probably why numbers like this were left off. Dave Mason helps out on guitar.

I FOUND A LOVE
(Unknown)

SOUNDING strangely incomplete, this outtake from the sessions for *There's One In Every Crowd* hardly features any guitar.

IT HURTS ME TOO
(London)

ANOTHER outtake from the *There's One...* sessions, this was probably left off because of the emphasis on Eric's guitar, but his blues playing is immaculate. This song was re-recorded for Eric's *From the Cradle* album.

WHATCHA GONNA DO
(Tosh)

ONE OF two reggae numbers recorded at Dynamic Sound Studios in Kingston with the for-mer Wailer Peter Tosh who was signed to Rolling Stones Records around this time. Intended for *There's One...* but left off because the album was eclectic enough already.

Eric: "Peter (Tosh) was weird. He would just be sitting in a chair – asleep or comatose. And then someone would count it off and he'd wake up and play, with that weird wah-wah reggae chop. And then at the end of the take he'd just nod off again!

"He didn't seem to know what the tune was, or it didn't matter. But then we'd get him to sing. He sang the pilot vocal to 'Burial', and also to 'Whatcha Gonna Do'. I couldn't understand a word. I literally couldn't! It was hard enough when those guys talked because you'd have to ask, 'Could you say that again *slowly* please.' But when they sang, it almost completely disappeared. Even today, I don't know if I sang the right words on that! I have no idea. And if I did, I don't know what half of them mean.

"We didn't release those two tracks because the feeling was that it was getting to be too much of a reggae thing. We'd just had a big hit with 'I Shot The Sheriff' and it was starting to become an overpowering influence. And there was a feeling of discontent amongst the band, too, that we were going off too much on a sidetrack, 'cause when we got onto the concert stage we weren't going to be a reggae band, so the album had to reflect what we were going to do live."

Peter Tosh was murdered during a burglary at his Kingston home in 1987.

FURTHER ON UP THE ROAD
(Veasey/Robey)

ERIC'S CONCERT at Hammersmith Odeon on April 27, 1977, was recorded with the intention of releasing a live double album that Christmas, but no material was released at the time. This is a guitarist extravaganza and despite interference from his amplifier, Eric plays his heart out.

HEAVEN IS ONE STEP AWAY
(Clapton)

ORIGINALLY recorded for *Behind The Sun* at Montserrat in the West Indies in 1984, this track was discarded when Eric's record company demanded that he record "more commercial" material. This great up-tempo track eventually found its way onto a 12" single as a bonus track, and it also turned up on the soundtrack for *Back To The Future*.

TOO BAD
(Clapton)

THIS MOURNFUL acoustic blues piece was also recorded during the *Behind The Sun* sessions

and rejected, probably because it's radically different from anything else recorded at the time. This also turned up as a 12" bonus track.

WANNA MAKE LOVE TO YOU
(Williams)

A SUPERB outtake from the *August* album sessions at Sunset Sound in Los Angeles during April 1986, this track was substituted at the last minute for the decidedly inferior 'It's In The Way That You Use It'. Eric clearly liked this song as he played it live and would introduce it in concert as "a number from my forthcoming album."

AFTER MIDNIGHT
(Cale)

A SHORT and controversial re-recording of one of Eric's most famous cover versions, which was used as the soundtrack to a beer commercial in America. Eric, of course, was an alcoholic at the time which he admitted later – to the beer company's chagrin. This version was only previously available as an unedited six minute take included on a giveaway cassette available through the beer company.

The Cream Of Eric Clapton

Polydor 521 881-2, released July 1994.

THE ORIGINAL COMPILATION, *THE CREAM OF ERIC CLAPTON* WAS DELETED and replaced with a new compilation carrying the same name in 1994. However, it's far from satisfactory and fans wanting a truer picture of Eric's work are directed to *Crossroads*. This record, which sticks rigidly to Eric's time on RSO Records, is only part of the story. Warner Brothers, for whom Eric has recorded since 1983, did not co-operate.

TRACKS: Layla, I Feel Free, Sunshine Of Your Love, Crossroads, Strange Brew, White Room, Bell Bottom Blues, Cocaine, I Shot the Sheriff, After Midnight, Swing Low Sweet Chariot, Lay Down Sally, Knockin' On Heaven's Door, Wonderful Tonight, Let It Grow, Promises, I Can't Stand It.

Crossroads 2

Universal 529305, released April 1996

1988'S *CROSSROADS* BOX SET ANTHOLOGY WAS SUCH A RUNAWAY success that it seemed logical to have a second volume. However, whilst the first set was largely a collection of greatest hits, alternative takes and the odd live cut from Clapton's career up to that point, *Crossroads 2* has a subtitle of 'Live In The Seventies'. The four disc set comprises a generous selection of live Clapton workouts from 1974 to 1978, most of which are previously unreleased. Clapton's live concerts have always been a perfect avenue for him to stretch out on the guitar, making the songs significantly different to their studio counterparts. The remarkable thing about this set is the fact that it was recorded during the height of Eric's drinking years. Unbelievably, he keeps it together and with the help of a strong band, turns out some genuinely inspired playing.

As a bonus, you also get a handful of unreleased studio tracks, one from the *461 Ocean Boulevard* sessions in 1974 and the others stem from a one-off session at Olympic Studios in 1978.

WALKIN' DOWN THE ROAD
(Levine/Musgrove)

ONE OF four studio cuts found on this otherwise live set. Recorded at Criteria Studios, Miami, in May 1974 during the *461 Ocean Boulevard* sessions. An inspired acoustic blues featuring Eric accompanied by Jamie Oldaker on drums and Carl Radle on bass. The sessions were the first since Eric's recovery from heroin addiction, so they were very much exploratory in terms of material. Many such songs were recorded along with lengthy blues instrumentals as the band got to know each other. A perfect introductory number for the next tune.

HAVE YOU EVER LOVED A WOMAN?
(Myles)

STRAIGHT into the live set now, with a stunning version of the Billy Myles classic which Eric had previously covered In the studio on the *Layla* album. This particular live version can also be found on *EC Was Here* but in a different mix. It was on the strength of this number that RSO were able to persuade Eric that an In-concert album would be a good idea. His guitar solo is probably one of the most inspired on this set. It was recorded at Long Beach Arena on July 19, 1974.

WILLIE AND THE HAND JIVE/GET READY
(Otis/Clapton/Elliman)

ORIGINALLY recorded at Criteria Studios in May 1974 and can be found on *461 Ocean Boulevard*. This live version also comes from Long Beach, albeit the next night. A perfect vehicle, Eric and Yvonne do get low down and dirty on this extended cut.

CAN'T FIND MY WAY HOME
(Winwood)

SAME VENUE as the previous number. This classic Blind Faith number is performed acoustically and is sung by Yvonne Elliman and Eric. It was a firm favourite during the 1974 US tour. At the conclusion of the song, you can hear Eric continuing to play and the band follow him into 'Driftin' Blues'.

DRIFTIN' BLUES/ RAMBLIN' ON MY MIND
(Moore/Brown/Williams/Johnson)

ORIGINALLY found on *EC Was Here*, you now get the remixed and remastered complete medley of the two songs. The US tours of 1974 and 1975 were particularly interesting in that the band would never play the same set twice. A lot of numbers that Eric would play were decided on the spot. This is one of those throw caution to the winds moments, and it works. Yes, there is some hesitation, particularly when Eric switches from acoustic to electric slide. But the overall feel is that of a band and its leader at one with each other. Recorded at Long Beach Arena on July 20, 1974.

PRESENCE OF THE LORD
(Clapton)

WRITTEN by Eric and originally cut with Blind Faith for their eponymous album, yet another song from the fine pair of Long Beach Arena shows that can also be found on *EC Was Here* in a different mix.

RAMBLIN' ON MY MIND/ HAVE YOU EVER LOVED A WOMAN?
(Johnson/Myles)

RECORDED at the first of two shows at London's Hammersmith Odeon on December 4, 1974, and also available in a different mix on *EC Was Here*.

LITTLE WING
(Hendrix)

ONE OF Jimi Hendrix's most hauntingly beautiful songs is performed here by Eric as a tribute to his friend. Although he had previously recorded it in the studio for the *Layla* album, it always sounded better live. This version is no exception. Also recorded at the Hammersmith show on December 4, it captures Eric in fine form playing his Gibson Explorer. Delicate vocals, sung in

unison by Eric and Yvonne, are punctuated by a sublime wah-wah solo. One of the many highlights of the two London shows.

THE SKY IS CRYING/ HAVE YOU EVER LOVED A WOMAN?/RAMBLIN' ON MY MIND
(James/Myles/Johnson)

ALTHOUGH the European tour of 1974 was still promoting *461 Ocean Boulevard*, Eric and his band had already recorded a follow-up album, *There's One In Every Crowd*. It was not due for release until April 1975, but Eric wanted to road test some of the songs to judge audience reactions. Elmore James' 'The Sky Is Crying' is just one of several new numbers from the forthcoming release that were performed during the tour. A slow, smouldering blues, it was played at the Hammersmith show as the first number of a medley which repeats 'Have You Ever Loved A Woman?' and 'Ramblin' On My Mind'.

LAYLA
(Clapton/Gordon)

ERIC WOULD open many of the 1975 shows with his best selling hit, 'Layla'. He played it as the opener as he was tired of fans shouting out for the number throughout the show. This way, he could get it out of the way and concentrate on the main set. The 1975 concert version did not include the piano coda found on the studio equivalent, but

Eric tears through the riff with an amazing solo that shows off his versatility on this fast paced favourite. Only two concerts were professionally recorded on the 1975 tour, and this number was recorded at Providence Civic Center on June 25.

FURTHER ON UP THE ROAD
(Veasey/Robey)

POPULARISED by Bobby Bland and one of Eric's most requested concert numbers for many years, this was the second song played on this particular evening and is probably not quite as good as the previously released version from the Nassau Coliseum (found on *EC Was Here*). Nonetheless, Eric and his band perform it with gusto.

I SHOT THE SHERIFF
(Marley)

RECORDED at Nassau Coliseum, Long Island, on June 28, 1975, this extended version of Eric's smash hit gives him ample opportunity to excel on the guitar. Eric and the band really get into a groove on this one. Probably the highlight of the whole set, confirming that the 1975 tour was one of Eric's best from that decade.

BADGE
(Clapton/Harrison)

STILL AT the Nassau gig, Eric and his band play 'Badge'. Of course,

the audience are waiting for the second half of the song, where Eric makes an all-out assault on guitar to the obvious delight of the crowd.

DRIFTIN' BLUES
(Moore/Brown/ Williams)

SIGNIFICANTLY different to the acoustic 1974 version found elsewhere on this set. This version is performed as a stand-alone, rather than in a medley, and on electric guitar. Recorded at Providence Civic Center.

EYESIGHT TO THE BLIND/ WHY DOES LOVE GOT TO BE SO SAD
(Williamson/Clapton/Whitlock)

ANOTHER highlight of the set. Santana were the support band on a large chunk of Eric's 1975 tour. Not surprisingly, Carlos would come out and join Eric for the encores to play another 30 plus minutes of extended jamming. The crowds went wild, and listening to these two numbers, it's easy to hear why. Again recorded at Providence Civic Center, Sonny Boy Williamson's 'Eyesight To The Blind' (as performed by Eric during his appearance in Ken Russell's film of The Who's *Tommy*, 1975) and the Dominos' favourite 'Why Does Love Got To Be So Sad', feature Eric and Carlos in a real guitar fest.

TELL THE TRUTH
(Clapton/Whitlock)

WE NOW jump to the Hammersmith Odeon in 1977. Eric and his band recorded two nights here with a view to releasing a double live album. It never happened, so here is a small opportunity to hear what they sounded like on the first of three tracks from the shows. 'Tell The Truth', originally due to be Derek & The Dominos' first studio single, was always a good excuse for a jam. Again, this extended version shows what a great band they were.

KNOCKIN' ON HEAVEN'S DOOR
(Dylan)

THE SECOND track from the 1977 Hammersmith Odeon. Eric had a hit single with this Dylan number back in 1975 and it was certainly a crowd pleaser performed with a light reggae lilt.

STORMY MONDAY
(Walker)

ALSO RECORDED at the Hammersmith Odeon in 1977, Eric is always at home on blues territory. T-Bone Walker's classic 'Stormy Monday Blues' is no exception and gives Clapton an opportunity to max out on the guitar.

LAY DOWN SALLY
(Clapton/Levy/Terry)

ANOTHER live favourite to get the clapping crowds on their feet. A simple JJ Cale-like shuffle, it was a huge hit for Eric. Recorded in 1978 at Santa Monica Civic Auditorium on the US 'Slowhand' tour.

THE CORE
(Clapton/Levy)

ALSO RECORDED at Santa Monica Civic Auditorium, this is a storming number with a recurring riff. Both Marcy and Eric handle vocal duties. The whole band cook on this one and Eric plays a demonic wah-wah solo. Another set highlight.

WE'RE ALL THE WAY
(Williams)

ERIC HAD a deep love of country artist Don Williams and his backing band, in particular, guitarist Danny Flowers. He would later cover Flowers' 'Tulsa Time', both in concert and in the studio. 'We're All The Way' is a gentle country ballad which is, frankly, out of place in concert. Yet another track from Santa Monica Civic Auditorium and originally recorded on the *Slowhand* album.

COCAINE
(Cale)

WHAT CAN one say about this classic live number? It's

hard to imagine Eric ever stopping playing this number live. This version is particularly good with a vibrant solo. Again from Santa Monica Civic Auditorium.

GOIN' DOWN SLOW/ RAMBLIN' ON MY MIND
(Oden/Johnson)

THIS WAS a set favourite during the US 1978 tour. Eric would often play a blues medley at this time, and this pairing works particularly well. 'Going Down Slow' starts lowdown and dirty with Eric soloing through the intro. Some genuinely superb playing here, and listen out for Eric's authentic vocals and flawless key changes as the band sway into 'Ramblin' On My Mind'. Stunning! (Recorded at Santa Monica Civic Auditorium).

MEAN OLD FRISCO
(Crudup)

ANOTHER blues classic with Eric in simply devastating form on slide, it's actually more enjoyable than the studio counterpart. Last number from the 1978 Santa Monica Civic Auditorium show.

LOVING YOU IS SWEETER THAN EVER
(Wonder/Hunter)

BACK IN Blighty for the Backless tour at the tail end of 1978, this classic Four Tops' Motown song, written by Stevie Wonder and Ivory Joe Hunter, was also covered by The Band. Eric absolutely loved this song and would often play it during soundchecks on this tour. Eventually he decided they should play it in the main set and this version opened the Victoria Hall, Hanley show. It was the first time the band had played it in front of a live audience. It wisely sticks to the original arrangement and features a respectful guitar solo.

WORRIED LIFE BLUES
(Merrweather)

THIS PIANO-driven blues number was a favourite in the late Seventies and early Eighties. Also from the Hanley concert.

TULSA TIME
(Flowers)

WRITTEN by Don Williams' guitarist, this number became a firm favourite with Eric and he would often dedicate it to his band, who originated from Tulsa. On this particular tour, the song was paired with 'Early In The Morning', just as it was on the *Backless* album. Eric plays some nifty slide on this. Recorded at Glasgow's famous Apollo Theatre.

EARLY IN THE MORNING
(Trad arr. Clapton)

THIS SONG would segue in from 'Tulsa Time' with Eric again providing some tasty slide work on this old traditional blues number. Recorded at Hanley.

WONDERUL TONIGHT
(Clapton)

PERHAPS his best known love song and an absolute 'must-play' concert favourite, this version is from the Apollo, Glasgow.

KIND HEARTED WOMAN
(Johnson)

THIS IMPROMPTU tribute to Robert Johnson was not on the set-list. Eric decided to play it after an audience member kept shouting out for some Robert Johnson. Taken from the Apollo, Glasgow.

DOUBLE TROUBLE
(Rush)

ERIC HAS cited Otis Rush as an early influence, so it was no surprise to hear him perform this number originally recorded for *No Reason To Cry* in 1976. 'Double Trouble' would remain a stage favourite for Eric during many tours, giving him an opportunity to jam with his band. This is a particularly fine version with some incredible jazzy interplay between all four band members. Recorded at the Victoria Hall, Hanley.

CROSSROADS
(Johnson)

OF COURSE, the definitive 'Crossroads' will always be the one found on Cream's *Wheels Of Fire*. This version, recorded at Hanley is a typical Seventies version and while it is still enjoyable, it's no match for the Cream masterpiece.

TO MAKE SOMEBODY HAPPY
(Clapton)

THE FIRST of three tracks recorded at Olympic Studios, London on 28 December, 1978. This was the first session with the English rhythm section comprising Dave Markee on bass and Henry Spinetti on drums. Eric had composed this number during his infamous Rolling Hotel train tour and can be seen in the rushes of the film playing it solo on acoustic guitar. Beautiful number with some subtle dobro and a sensitive electric solo.

CRYIN'
(Clapton)

THE SECOND number is a simple acoustic blues that is similar in vein to 'Key To The Highway'. Eric is in fine voice.

WATER ON THE GROUND
(Clapton)

THE THIRD and last number from the Olympic sessions; a sensitive acoustic ballad with some pleasant dreamlike qualities to it. On the strength of these three numbers, the band should have recorded a full album, but only these three numbers were attempted.

Clapton Chronicles:
Best Of

Reprise 9362475642, released October 1999

THE *CLAPTON CHRONICLES* **ALBUM COVERS THE WARNERS PART OF HIS CAREER,** from 1981 through to 1999, but bizarrely manages to ignore his first album for the label, *Money And Cigarettes*. Also ignored is the triple-platinum blues album *From The Cradle*. So what you get on this compilation is Eric veering predominantly into pop territory and this collection captures some of the best songs from this period. Because they could not use material from the RSO years, Warners used several of his early classics from live shows in the Nineties, such as 'Layla' from the *Unplugged* album. *Chronicles* is squarely aimed at the pop market. Fans wanting to get a fuller picture of Eric's hits would be better served with Crossroads.

BLUE EYES BLUE
(Warren)

TAKEN from the film soundtrack *The Runaway Bride*, starring Julia Roberts and Richard Gere. The chords for this pleasant acoustic ditty are simplistic, Eric plays the E in a D shape on the 4th fret and all the other chords as bar chords so no open strings. He also uses his classic "thumb over neck" for the bass strings on bar chords. He used his Martin 00028EC signature model.

CHANGE THE WORLD
(Kennedy/Kirkpatrick/Sims)

ANOTHER soundtrack number, this time from the John Travolta film, *Phenomenon*. The vocals on this cut are outstanding with a wonderful soulful vibe, helped no doubt by the Babyface production. Eric's vocals definitely changed and improved from the late Nineties onwards.

(I) GET LOST
(Clapton)

THE THIRD soundtrack number on this compilation from *The Story Of Us*. Ironically, the acoustic original found on the soundtrack is the better bet than this more dance oriented version.

Eric Clapton: The Blues

Universal 5471782, released July 1999

*E*RIC CLAPTON: THE BLUES IS A TWO DISC COMPILATION OF LARGELY previously released material, comprising one disc of studio tracks and one side of live material. As the title says, the main emphasis here is on the blues. The studio material found on Disc One is drawn from Eric's lesser known albums, while the live material found on the second disc provides a strong selection of Eric in concert between 1974 and 1978. One of the highlights on the first disc is 'Have You Ever Loved A Woman?' from the *Layla And Assorted Love Songs* double. Another is the *461 Ocean Boulevard* outtake, 'Ain't That Loving You' which has some fine slide playing on it.

The live disc is largely sourced from *Crossroads 2*, along with two songs from the *Just One Night* double live set, and one previously unreleased. 'Have You Ever Loved A Woman?' is one of the better songs showing great control of sustain. From a commercial point of view, Universal felt obliged to include Eric's love ballad 'Wonderful Tonight', but it does stand out like a sore thumb among all the blues numbers.

For Eric Clapton fans wishing to acquaint themselves with his blues work, this is an excellent place to start.

Disc 1 - Studio

BEFORE YOU ACCUSE ME
(McDaniel)

CLASSIC Bo Diddley tune which Eric recorded during sessions for *Backless* in August 1978. Eric did later record another version for his 1989 *Journeyman* album but this previously unreleased version is vastly different. A rollicking shuffle that is arguably better than the '89 version.

MEAN OLD WORLD
(Jacobs)

AN AMAZING take recorded during sessions for the *Layla* album. Eric and Duane Allman in impassioned mode with a simple backbeat from drummer Jim Gordon.

ALBERTA
(Trad arr. Ledbetter)

A PREVIOUSLY unreleased solo performance recorded during the *Slowhand* sessions in 1977. This would be played regularly during the '77 tour, so it's surprising it was left off the original album, although Eric's vocals do sound the worse for wear. This version pretty much sticks to Ledbelly's original arrangement. He would also later play this on his *Unplugged* session in 1992.

DOWN IN THE BOTTOM
(Dixon)

O NE OF many previously unreleased blues numbers recorded for *461 Ocean Boulevard* in 1974. The band sound tight and get a moody groove going before Eric starts singing.

BEFORE YOU ACCUSE ME
(McDaniel)

T HE SECOND take of this number which is also previously unreleased from the 1978 *Backless* sessions. This take is a completely different arrangement to the first version which opens this compilation. Eric shouts out the count-in and the band take off on this lively shuffle.

Disc 2 - Live

FURTHER ON UP THE ROAD
(Veasey/Robey)

R ECORDED live in Dallas on 15 November 1976 for a *King Biscuit Flower Hour* radio broadcast and previously released on an out-of-print Freddie King album, 1934 – 76. Sadly, it never made the radio show and this is now the only place to find this number. A classic jam between Eric and Freddie King, who had recently signed with RSO, Eric's label at the time.

PART SEVEN
SOUNDTRACKS & SESSION WORK

THROUGHOUT THE EIGHTIES AND NINETIES, ERIC CLAPTON ALSO MADE HIS presence felt in the world of television and film soundtracks. His first dedicated contribution was to the marvellous BBC drama production, *Edge Of Darkness*, in 1985. Eric provided the whole soundtrack, including incidental music, and he recorded it at Pete Townshend's Eel Pie Studios while watching the images on a monitor screen. He managed to capture the essence of this tense thriller with some hauntingly expressive guitar work.

His next major soundtrack was for the first of the hugely popular 'buddy films', *Lethal Weapon*, which starred Danny Glover and Mel Gibson. Yet again, Eric's captivating guitar work adds to the general excitement of what you are seeing on screen. His incidental guitar work is truly mesmerising. He went on to do all the *Lethal Weapon* soundtracks. Later on Eric contributed to such movies as *Rush*, *Back To The Future*, *The Color Of Money* and *The Story Of Us*. His greatest soundtrack success, however, came with 'Change The World', the endearing smash hit from the John Travolta film *Phenomenon*.

You can be sure that more soundtrack work awaits him when time permits.

GUEST SESSIONS

ERIC CLAPTON'S WILLING PARTICIPATION IN EXTRACURRICULAR SESSION work is well documented. He has performed on well over one hundred albums by other artists over the years. It provides him with an opportunity to play in a different environment to his own, and helps his creativity. It's almost impossible to list them all, and Eric himself has probably forgotten many of them, some of his more memorable sessions are listed here.

His first ever session was for an Otis Spann single in May 1964, when he was still with The Yardbirds and this gave him a taste of a different world. Eric's love of the blues meant that an opportunity to play with the real deal was a dream come true, especially as this was Eric's first meeting with Muddy Waters, who was playing guitar on the session. Eric remembers it well, "Muddy was playing rhythm guitar and I played lead, which was strange, and it was two sides we did with Mike Vernon. And it was great, actually. They were both very friendly, you know, very encouraging. And they had these beautiful shiny silk suits, with big trousers. I was knocked out by the way they looked."

Not long after joining John Mayall's Bluesbreakers in April 1965, Eric got to play on a rare UK session by Bob Dylan at Levy's Recording Studio in London. Sadly, the version of 'If You Gotta Go, Go Now' remains unreleased.

Another early session for Eric was one which made him incredibly nervous. Cream were recording tracks for their forthcoming *Wheels Of Fire* album at Atlantic Studios in New York and Jerry Wexler suggested to Eric that he might want to drop in on a session for a new Aretha Franklin record. Eric layed down a beautifully expressive blues solo on a track called 'Good To Me As I Am To You', which appeared on Aretha's *Lady Soul* album.

His best known Sixties appearance is on The Beatles' 1968 double 'White Album' (a.k.a. *The Beatles*), where he plays the guitar solo on George Harrison's 'While My Guitar Gently Weeps'. The Beatles did not normally invite guests to play on their records, and it's now common knowledge that George invited him to the session in an attempt to reduce some of the tension that was growing between the members of the group during these sessions. The original guitar solo, not surprisingly, sounded too much like Eric Clapton and not sufficiently like The Beatles. To give it that authentic Beatles sound, they fed the guitar through an ADT machine, Harrison recalling that they "put it (Eric's guitar) through the automatic double-tracker, to wobble it a bit. The drums would be all on one track, bass on another, the acoustic on another, piano on another, Eric on another, and the vocal on another, and then whatever else. I sang it with the acoustic guitar with Paul on piano, and Eric and Ringo. Later, Paul ovedubbed bass on it."

Eric's last high profile guest appearance in the Sixties was for The Rolling Stones film, *Rock And Roll Circus*, in December 1968. He played on two numbers with a superstar band calling themselves The Dirty Mac. The group comprised John Lennon on guitar, Yoko Ono on vocals, Mitch Mitchell on drums, Keith Richards on bass and Eric on lead guitar. The film was shelved due to the Stones supposedly lacklustre performance, but was eventually released in 1996 on video (2004 on DVD) as well as on the accompanying soundtrack. Eric contributes some heavy licks to Lennon's 'Yer Blues'. The other track, 'Whole Lotta Yoko' was an instrumental piece featuring Yoko Ono's primal screams and of no real interest to fans of Clapton, except maybe to raise a smile!

Clapton's and Lennon's paths crossed again the following year when John invited Eric to play with The Plastic Ono Band at the Toronto Rock 'n' Roll Revival Concert on September 13, 1969 (released in December as *Live Peace In Toronto* 1969, Apple Records) and on the recording session of Lennon's latest song, the harrowing 'Cold Turkey', released October 1969 as an Apple single. Eric, with George Harrison and Delaney, Bonnie & Friends also took part in an all-star ad-hoc colossus formed for a UNICEF benefit at London's Lyceum in December 1969, playing two songs, 'Cold Turkey' and 'Don't Worry Kyoko (Mummy's Only Looking For Her Hand In The Snow)' which Lennon later released as Side Three of the *Some Time In New York City* double album in 1972 (Apple Records).

In a further Beatle connection, Eric spent part of the late Sixties lending his guitar skills to various newly signed artists to the Apple label, most notably Jackie Lomax ('Sour Milk Sea', Apple, 1968 and the *Is This What You Want?* album, 1969) and Billy Preston (*That's The Way God Planned It*, 1969). He would not be credited on the sleeve of these albums to save any potential contractual difficulties. His first major session of note at this time was in the summer of 1970 for George Harrison's post Beatles masterpiece, *All Things Must Pass*. Eric contributed to most tracks and the sessions would lead him to form Derek & The Dominos. By the time the Dominos hit the road later in the year, he did not have much time for guest spots. After May 1971, he became a recluse in the Surrey countryside having become dependent on heroin.

Apart from appearing at the two Bangla Desh benefit concerts on August 1, 1971, Eric re-emerged in 1974 in a blaze of publicity. His first session that year was with The Who on the soundtrack for their forthcoming Ken Russell-produced version of *Tommy*. Eric played on a mediocre 'Sally Simpson' which was more than compensated by an exhilarating 'Eyesight To The Blind' which Eric would later perform in concert on the 1975 tour.

He would spend a lot of the rest of the year and 1975 on tour and in the studio. But he found time to appear on a session for his friend Bob Dylan in July 1975 for Dylan's *Desire* album. Not a brilliant session for Eric as only one track, 'Romance In Durango', ended up being released. Eric recalled that... "it was very hard to keep up with him. He wasn't sure what he wanted. He was really looking, racing from song to song." That explains it then.

When working on his *No Reason To Cry* album in April 1976, Eric found the time to play on several sessions for people such as Joe Cocker, Stephen Bishop and Rick Danko, to name a few.

One of Eric's most enjoyable sessions was for his blood brother, Ronnie Lane in February 1977. Together with Pete Townshend, they recorded four tracks together which were released on that year's excellent Townshend-Lane *Rough Mix* collaboration.

Eric continued to contribute to various sessions throughout the Eighties, but the most significant was for the Roger Waters album, *The Pros And Cons Of Hitch Hiking* in 1983. Perhaps not an obvious pairing, Eric actually played on the whole album and enjoyed the experience so much he went out on tour in Waters' band in 1984 to tour the album. Eric had reached stagnation point with his own music and needed to simply be a guitarist in a band with no responsibilities.

Another unusual pairing was a session Eric did with Lionel Ritchie for his *Dancing On The Ceiling* album. Evidently the two had met each other on a fishing trip, and Lionel invited Eric to play on the track 'Tonight Will Be Alright'.

The late Eighties saw Eric play on albums by artists as diverse as Sting, Leona Boyd, Jon Astley and Jack Bruce. Eric ended up playing on two tracks on his old Cream partner's album, *Willpower*. It showed that there was still some magic between the two, and Eric would play on further sessions with him later.

His next significant session was for Elton John's *The One* album. Eric played and sang on 'Runaway Train', a big hit single for them in 1992. They also toured together as joint headliners around the world that year. Eric would continue to participate on other artists' sessions throughout the Nineties and in the Noughties by people as diverse as Brian Wilson, The Rolling Stones, Taj Mahal, Kate Bush, Toots & The Maytals, The Crickets, Buddy Guy, Marcus Miller, The Crusaders and Ringo Starr amongst others.

Finally, a year after the death of his close friend George Harrison in November 2001, Eric was invited by Harrison's widow Olivia to be the musical director for an all-star concert at London's Royal Albert Hall celebrating Harrison's music. In this capacity Eric led a band that on various numbers included Paul McCartney, Ringo Starr, Jeff Lynne, Tom Petty, Albert Lee, Klaus Voorman, Ray Cooper, Jim Keltner, Jim Capaldi, Jules Holland, Andy Fairthweather-Low, Billy Preston, Joe Brown and George's son Dhani. The emotion-tinged concert is available on DVD and as a live double CD.

Index